BEYOND TRANS

Beyond Trans

Does Gender Matter?

Heath Fogg Davis

NEW YORK UNIVERSITY PRESS

New York

NEW YORK UNIVERSITY PRESS
New York
www.nyupress.org

© 2017 by New York University
All rights reserved

References to Internet websites (URLs) were accurate at the time of writing. Neither the author nor New York University Press is responsible for URLs that may have expired or changed since the manuscript was prepared.

ISBN: 978-1-4798-5540-7

For Library of Congress Cataloging-in-Publication data, please contact the Library of Congress.

New York University Press books are printed on acid-free paper, and their binding materials are chosen for strength and durability. We strive to use environmentally responsible suppliers and materials to the greatest extent possible in publishing our books.

Manufactured in the United States of America

10 9 8 7 6 5 4 3 2 1

Also available as an ebook

For my kids

CONTENTS

Introduction

Sex Stickers

It was another day of using a city bus to get around Philadelphia. The Southeastern Pennsylvania Transportation Authority runs public transportation in this city of a million and a half. People here just call it SEPTA. And everyone has a SEPTA story to share, or maybe two or three. The buses, trains, and trolleys that crisscross the city are notoriously late and crowded. The company slogan, "We're getting there," says it all. It's as if the ad writers knew they had to keep it real in this city of grit.

Charlene Arcila, an African American transgender woman who lived and died in this city, was no stranger to grit.[1] For her it was another day of dealing with the snickers and sneers of the people she passed on sidewalks and interacted with in stores and restaurants. On top of all that, there were the sex stickers. She swiped her monthly public transit pass marked with an F to signify a female sex sticker, and braced for what might come. She hoped that she could quietly find a seat, and ride to where she needed to go. That today would be one of the good days in the "city of brotherly love." It was not. Arcila tells her story in a weary voice.

> The driver was like, "You cannot use this pass." After I had swiped it, and as I was walking to my seat, he called me back to the front and I said, "Well, why can't I?" He said, "Because you are not a female." And I was like, "Well, I am a transsexual." And he's like, "What's that?!" And I'm like, okay, I do not feel like educating this man right now. I just want to get to my destination. So I pulled out two dollars, and I put the two dollars into the meter.[2]

On a subsequent bus trip, Arcila tried to use an M for male transit pass. It, too, was rejected, this time on the bus driver's pronouncement that she was not a male.

From 1981 to July of 2013, SEPTA mandated that all of its monthly transit passes bear a male or female sticker that matched the sex identity of its purchaser and user. SEPTA's employee handbook instructed bus operators to verify each monthly pass for the correct date and the correct sex marker. But the handbook gave no guidance about the criteria that bus drivers should use to verify the sex of riders as they carried out their many other stressful duties. Consequently, individual bus operators were free to use their own subjective sex-identity judgments to determine which pass holders could access the buses under their control.

Having had both her female and male sex-marked passes rejected, Arcila, a longtime activist for transgender and gay rights in Philadelphia, filed a formal legal complaint with the city of Philadelphia. The complaint alleged that SEPTA's sex sticker policy violated her civil right to be free of "gender identity" discrimination. The city added "gender identity" to its lengthy list of legally protected identity categories in 2002. The ordinance defines gender identity as "self-perception, or perception by others, as male or female," which includes "an individual's appearance, behavior, or physical characteristics, that may be in accord with, or opposed to one's physical anatomy, chromosomal sex, or sex assigned at birth; and shall include, but not be limited to, individuals who are undergoing or have completed sex reassignment."[3]

The discrimination being pinpointed here, in my view, is more accurately described as *sex-identity* discrimination because it involves judgments about whether a person belongs to the sex categories of male or female. By contrast, traditional sexism is based on judgments about what we can and cannot do *because* we are male or female. These "scripts for identity" are what we commonly refer to as *gender* stereotypes.[4]

SEPTA instituted the sex sticker policy in 1981 as a fraud-prevention measure aimed to deter the swapping of passes between husbands and wives sharing a household.[5] Fraud prevention is a legitimate business goal. But the male or female stickers were not rationally related to that goal because females could share their passes with other females, and males could share their passes with other males, both within and without heterosexual households. Some commuter railroads such as New York's Metro Transit Authority Long Island and Metro North Railroad sex-mark their passes, but SEPTA was the only noncommuter transit authority to sex-mark its monthly passes. Like SEPTA, the MTA cites fraud prevention as the reason for its sex marker policy.[6]

Why did SEPTA riders tolerate this irrational practice, and why do MTA riders in New York continue to tolerate it? But when you think about it, maybe the policy is not so unusual. After all, most of us carry other sex-marked identity documents in our pockets and purses—be it a driver's license, state identification card, or passport.

Ripple Effects

Arcila was not the first or only person to have her sex-marked transit pass rejected by a bus operator. Other bus riders whose appearances also challenged prevailing gender norms reported having been questioned and harassed by bus operators when they attempted to use their transit passes. SEPTA and Philadelphia's Commission on Human Relations, the official body charged with enforcing the city's Fair Practices Ordinance, had received numerous complaints about SEPTA's gender sticker policy.

In 2009, a local grassroots organization called R.A.G.E. (Riders Against Gender Exclusion) sprouted to bring public attention to the invidious impact of SEPTA's sex-identity sticker policy. The organization solicited and compiled its own catalogue of sex-identity discrimination stories from SEPTA bus riders. R.A.G.E. used social media to collect and publicize stories that vividly portrayed the widespread harm done by the stickers. The stories flooded in both from people who self-identified as transgender and those who did not, as well as from riders who self-identified as queer and those who did not.

One woman with short hair recounted her experience of being sold a male-marked monthly pass unbeknownst to her at the time she purchased it at a ticket window. She became aware of the ticket salesperson's mistake the next day when she tried to use her male-marked pass and the bus operator accused her of fraud, and tried to confiscate her eighty-three-dollar pass. Another female rider said a bus operator mistook her for male based on her appearance. When he noticed her female-marked pass, he realized his mistake. But instead of apologizing for his error, he verbally harassed her and confiscated her pass. Several transgender women shared stories similar to Arcila's. They had tried to use a female pass only to have the card denied because the operator did not think they "counted as a woman."[7]

Other gender-nonconforming riders described being verbally harassed and sometimes even physically intimidated by other riders when they overheard a bus operator loudly questioning their gender identity. Christian A'Xavier Lovehall, a black transgender man, described an incident that occurred prior to his gender transition, when he self-identified as a butch lesbian. Like Arcila, he was called back to the front of the bus after swiping his transit pass. In his words,

I came back, and he says, "You can't use this." And I'm like what are you talking about? "You can't use this transpass." So I'm like, "Why?" So, he's looking at me, but he's hearing me 'cause out of my mouth is coming a female voice, but he sees a young boy. To him, he sees a young boy. And so he just looks at me with this startled face, and says, "What are you?" And I was young, so I answered him. I said, "I'm a girl." And he continued to stare at me with disbelief and didn't say anything else. And you know I'm not gonna just stand here while you stare at me. So I proceeded to walk to back of the bus. And he continued to stare at me . . . through the mirror to the back of the bus. And [he] did not move the bus yet. That causes everybody on the bus now to look at me. Now I hear comments from the passengers. "Why doesn't she shave her legs? I understand she's a lesbian but at least shave your legs."[8]

The question "What are you?" is demeaning. It refers to an object, not a person. The legitimate question when proffering any identity document is "*Who* are you?" But the sex stickers detracted from that inquiry by focusing on sex.

Many other transgender and gender-nonconforming transit pass holders also recounted traumatic stories of verbal abuse and physical intimidation by other passengers after a bus driver had questioned them about their sex identity. Max Ray, a white transgender man and R.A.G.E. member, vividly recalled his own very bad day on SEPTA.

> I went to swipe my pass, and there was three or four teenage guys on the front of the trolley and they started saying, "That's a female. That's a female. They think that's a female. You're a he-she." And just things going on from there. And I, again, felt very intimidated. They got off before I did, which was lucky for me, I think. But I don't know what I would have done if they had gotten off at my stop. Or if I had gotten off, I thought they might follow me off.

Street harassment is part of everyday life in a city for people whose appearances challenge prevailing gender norms.

At thirty-eight, Arcila was a veteran. Being verbally harassed and physically intimidated in public had long been familiar—so familiar that she had built her own mental coat of armor that she donned frequently while out in public. When the bus drivers loudly questioned her sex identity and the other passengers stared and chimed in with their own judgments, Arcila said, "I found myself [again] locked in that protective zone of blackening everybody around me out of my vision."[9]

There were tales, too, of the basic humiliation of having to walk up to a ticket window and ask for a *female* or *male* transit pass in a society where our maleness or femaleness is supposed to be visually obvious to those who see and interact with us in public. As Nico Amador, a R.A.G.E. member, explains, many non-transgender people were questioned about their sex-marked passes, too. There are many reasons why a person might appear to be androgynous, such as "an older person whose appearance was a little more ambiguous. I think the same thing happens with youth a lot of the time, and there's a lot of people out there who just present more androgynously for one reason or another."[10] What is clear from these testimonials is that both the ticket window agents issuing the passes and the bus operators charged with verifying their "correctness" had tremendous power over SEPTA riders. They literally had the last word about the customer's sex identity.

In addition to collecting vivid testimonials of the pain and suffering wrought by the seemingly innocuous sex-identity stickers, R.A.G.E. employed a mix of traditional and innovative protest strategies to draw public attention to the issue of "gender identity" discrimination. They staged a rally-style drag show at SEPTA's busy city hall subway with the cheeky name "SEPTA is a Drag!" At the rally, R.A.G.E. protestors carried signs saying, "Stop Gender Policing and Discrimination," "Feel free to check my crotch," and "SEPTA is full of cissies."

The organization penned a Riders' Bill of Rights that stated in part, "We have the right not to be forced into the categories of male or female." They disrupted public hearings to read it out loud. They gathered thousands of signatures on a petition that its members presented to SEPTA's general manager, Joe Casey. Initially, Casey agreed to discontinue the sticker policy, but then prevaricated and failed to do so for over three years.[11] Finally, in the eighth paragraph of an eleven-paragraph May 23, 2013, media release about fare increases, SEPTA quietly announced that it would end its sex-identity sticker policy effective July 1, 2013.[12]

The demise of the sex sticker policy was a victory for R.A.G.E. The group worked tirelessly and creatively to push SEPTA to the point that it finally gave in. But the victory was bittersweet because SEPTA never conceded that its gender sticker policy caused "gender identity" discrimination.[13] That, in my view, was the radical essence of Arcila's legal complaint. It's true that the complaint did not invoke constitutional rights or statutory law, and so it would not have established a legal precedent in either of those senses. Still, the legal complaint had the potential to set an important precedent for bringing to light the basic fact that sex-classification policies *cause* sex-identity discrimination.

Commenting on the SEPTA gender sticker case, Harper Jean Tobin, then a lawyer and now the policy director at the National Center for Transgender Equality, told the press, "So many times in the past, a government or bureaucratic system created a policy in which gender was unthinkingly made a part of a document or a database, with unintended consequences such as this." But instead of radically questioning our need for sex-classification policies, Tobin endorsed policy changes to make it easier for people who change their sex identities from male to female or female to male to have that change reflected on their sex-marked birth certificates, driver's licenses, and passports.[14] What made the gender sticker case so radical and important, in my view, was the use of antidiscrimination law to challenge the need for bureaucratic sex classification itself.

Personal Resonance

The sex sticker case interested me as both a political theorist and someone involved in transgender activism in Philadelphia. But Arcila's story also struck a personal note with me. As a transgender man who transitioned at the age of thirty-eight, I'd had decades of bruising encounters with sex-classification policies.

I was also a Philadelphia public transit rider who relied on SEPTA to commute to work and to get around my city. But unlike Arcila and many other Philly residents, I did not have to commute to my job five days a week, and so it was more cost-effective for me to buy tokens than to purchase monthly passes. This allowed me to avoid the direct effects of the gender stickers. And even if I had needed to use public transportation every day, I had the financial means to forego a monthly pass and thereby avoid the sex stickers. So I witnessed the controversy from a class-privileged perch.

But the witnessing unleashed hard memories. As a "tomboy" who preferred and was allowed by my parents to wear boy's clothing, and keep a short haircut, I was routinely questioned and reprimanded by girls and women for being in the "wrong" public bathroom. Yet, I did not feel entitled to use a male-designated restroom. No one ever gave me permission to do so. Like many other gender-nonconforming children, I learned through repeated scolding that the public sphere was not fully open to me because of the binary sex classification signs posted on just about every public bathroom door.

Later, post-puberty, the reprimands continued but depending upon what I was wearing and the length of my hair, I could sometimes defend my right to be in a female-designated restroom by speaking. My high-pitched "female" voice was mostly taken as sufficient proof that I was in the "right" restroom. Depending on my clothing, sometimes the accuser saw that I had female breasts. When this happened, my accuser was sometimes embarrassed and apologetic, but not always. Even when I was vindicated, it did not always mean that I was accepted or welcomed. Like Lovehall's account of being stared at by the bus driver and the other passengers after saying "I'm a girl," my declaration often intensified the staring and recalcitrance of my inquisitor.

The last time I used a women's restroom was in Heathrow Airport in the summer of 2008. I had just begun my gender-transition process, but had yet to start the testosterone therapy that would gradually masculinize my voice and appearance over the course of about three years. Ahead of me, too, was a bilateral mastectomy that is commonly referred to as "top surgery" in the transgender male community. My girlfriend and I were on our way to a summer vacation in Spain, and this was our second layover. It had been a stressful trip already. On the first layover in Frankfurt we learned that none of our luggage had made it out of Miami. It appeared we would be enjoying our two-week vacation with what we were wearing. And we had many hours to kill before embarking upon the final leg of our journey.

Jet-lagged, I made the best of my first-world problem by sauntering into a fancy airport store for English gents to buy some overpriced boxer shorts. After that, I walked into a women's restroom, hoping that this would be one of the "okay" times when no one hassled me. At the sink, while washing my hands and seeing tired eyes in the mirror, a female-appearing janitor approached. I could see a quiet storm brewing in her facial features. Her words to me: "You do realize this is a women's bathroom, don't you?" I met her comment with my own Canadian version of quiet sternness: "You do realize that I'm a woman, don't you?"

The next time that nature called, I headed to the men's restroom. My heart was pounding in my ears. I briskly made my way to an empty stall, peed, washed my hands, and left. No one stared at me. No one asked me whether I was aware that I was in a men's restroom. Indeed, no one seemed to even notice that I was there. As my sex-identity transition progressed, the use of men's rooms became easier and easier for me, except for those damn urinals, which I could not use. It has now been nine years since my Heathrow farewell to the women's room—exactly the number of years since I was last interrogated and reprimanded for taking care of my bodily functions in public. Now, as a transgender man whose appearance conforms to masculine gender norms, I always use men's restrooms, and I am never questioned while doing so.

I have mixed feelings about this newfound freedom. On one hand, it's great to be able to relieve myself in public restrooms without constantly bracing myself for the onslaught of inquisition and humiliation. On the other hand, I know all too well that this easement is one of the many concessions given to men who conform to the prevailing masculine norms in dress, hairstyle, and behavior. For anyone who has ever wondered if girls' and women's appearance and behavior are policed in ways that gender-conforming boys and men never experience, the answer is a resounding and sad yes. It is one thing to know these things as a girl and later as a woman. But it is another thing to experience such things from the other side of the sex binary.

Transgender women who have lived significant portions of their lives as male experience an opposite crossing-over effect. They turn in their "man card" and lose the patriarchal privileges that it bestowed. In her book *Whipping Girl*, transgender activist Julia Serano explores how US culture's "fascination with feminization" shapes the images we see of transgender women in popular culture. The marketing hook of most fictional and documentary stories about transgender identity is to "catch trans women *in the act* of putting on lipstick, dresses, and high heels, thereby giving the audience the impression that the trans woman's femaleness is an artificial mask or costume." If the "costume" is convincing, the narrative spin is deception. If not, then the narrative spin is comic failure: the pathetic "man in a dress."[15]

Public restrooms and public transportation are very different public spaces, but I am struck by what the sex-classification policies regulating these two venues have in common. Both sex-segregated restrooms and sex-marked bus passes create scenarios whereby employees are granted the power to evaluate our sex identities. And both policies prompt the inherently demeaning question of "what" we are instead of the sometimes legitimate question of "who" we are. It is easy to see the faulty logic in SEPTA's rationale for its sex stickers. Most people would agree that bus operators should not be inspecting the sex identities of bus riders. But should the janitor cleaning restrooms at Heathrow Airport have been given the authority to evaluate my sex identity?

In both scenarios the employees also had the discretionary leeway not to play the part of gender inspectors. Indeed, many SEPTA bus operators chose not to enforce the sex-sticker policy, even though the employee handbook told them to do so. Similarly, there are many janitors, and other employees in restaurants, airports, schools, and other public spaces who see transgender and gender-nonconforming people and do not feel the need to question whether they know which bathroom they are in. The problem is that these administrative agents have the power to do so if they so choose.

Naming the Problem

The administrative discretion to decide who is female and who is male is the essence of sex-identity discrimination, which I define as a specific subcategory of sexism. As previously discussed, I use the term "sex identity" instead of the term "gender identity" because I think it more accurately describes the source of this particular kind of sexism: judgments about who does and does not belong in the sex categories of male or female. By contrast, sex-based disadvantage occurs when gender stereotypes are used to limit what a person can and cannot do because she *is* a woman, or he *is* a man. All people who experience sex-identity discrimination also experience gender stereotyping.

However, not everyone who experiences gender stereotyping experiences sex-identity discrimination. When people speak of "transgender discrimination" they are really talking about sex-identity discrimination. But the term "transgender discrimination" is a misnomer because not all transgender people are vulnerable to "transgender discrimination," and some people who are not transgender are vulnerable to "transgender discrimination." Recall that some non-transgender women with short hair were issued male-marked SEPTA passes because they were wrongly perceived to be men, and as a gender-conforming transgender man, my use of men's restrooms has never been questioned.

These definitions are important to keep in mind when it comes to making sense of transgender discrimination statistics, most of which are based upon surveys of people who *self-identify* as transgender. This means that the rates of sex-identity discrimination are likely even higher than these surveys convey. A 2011 national transgender discrimination survey found transgender respondents reported alarmingly high rates of harassment, violence, and discrimination in education, employment, housing, treatment by police and in prison, and health care. The unemployment rate for transgender people is double that for non-transgender people. Transgender people of color experienced a rate of unemployment four times the national rate. When the intersecting factors of race and class and the direction of sex-identity transition (i.e., male to female, or female to male) are taken into account, the statistical picture of transgender discrimination and violence becomes even grimmer. The statistical picture for transgender women of color is especially dire.[16]

In addition to these grim statistics about accessing primary social goods, transgender and gender-nonconforming people have more difficulty than non-transgender people in sustaining life itself. Transgender and gender-nonconforming people, especially youth, have higher suicide rates and higher homicide rates than their non-transgender counterparts. The 2011 survey showed that 40 percent of anti-LGBT murder victims were transgender women.[17] Black and Latina transgender women are murdered at higher rates than white transgender women, and their murders are especially brutal and typified by overkill.

Police departments often fail to adequately investigate such murders, in large part because the murders of transgender people fail to garner the mainstream media attention that would pressure law enforcement officials to be more accountable to the public they serve. And when such murders are reported, many journalists describe transgender women as men, use their given male names instead of their chosen female names, and print pre-sex-identity-transition photos of them. These actions not only fail to accord slain transgender women dignity, but also impede police investigation by making them unrecognizable to anyone who may have witnessed their murders.[18]

Poor black and Latina transgender women are often targeted, harassed, and arrested by police officers under the stereotypical assumption that they are prostitutes. New York City's "stop and frisk" policy facilitated this kind of intersectional racial profiling, but black and Latina transgender women were never featured alongside the black and Latino non-transgender men that mainstream media focused on to highlight the policy's disparate race-sex impact.[19] This can be viewed as an extension of the "necropolitics" of black gendered embodiment that political theorist Shatema Threadcraft describes in her poignant characterization of how the state creates and perpetuates a black death world in which the murders of black women go largely unseen.[20]

This crisis of actual homicide exists alongside innumerable popular culture depictions of violence against "deceptive" transgender women. As Serano recounts in her analysis of misogyny directed at transgender

women in US television and film, "While the 'deceiver' is initially perceived to be a 'real' female, she is eventually revealed as a wolf in sheep's
clothing—an illusion that is the product of lies and modern medical
technology—and she is usually punished accordingly."[21]

Transgender and gender-nonconforming people bear the brunt of
sex-identity discrimination. However, people who are "cisgender" (a
term used to describe a person who does not self-identify as transgender) are also harmed by sex-classification policies. They are harmed on
an existential level because such policies constrict everyone's personal
freedom to imagine and define not just our gender expression of masculinity and femininity, but also our authority to make self-regarding
decisions about our sex identities—about who we are in relation to the
categories of male and female. This existentialist sex-based harm also
has serious practical consequences, as in, for example, when a caregiver
is unable to enter a sex-segregated public accommodation such as a restroom or locker room to assist a different-sex person in his or her care.
As I make plain, sex-classification policies are a major source of constraint, both externally and internally, on all of us.

Here, There, Everywhere

The high number and wide range of sex-classification policies that
govern our individual and social lives are profound. And in the same
way that governments and other institutions have "unthinkingly made
gender part of a document or a database," many of us follow these sex-
classification policies without giving them much thought.

For instance, most people see the signs on public restroom doors and
obey them. There are rule breakers, of course. Sometimes this is because
the person disagrees with the rule. Sometimes the person agrees with
the rule, but must violate it out of necessity, as in the case of a parent out
in public with an opposite-sex child. When I take my eleven-month-old
daughter into a men's restroom with me to change her diaper, I violate
the "male-only" rule governing that space.

Some establishments have two single-user bathrooms, and label one for women and the other for men. I am always amazed to see people waiting for "their" single-user sex-marked bathroom to become free, as the door to the other single-user sex-marked bathroom is wide open. But at the same time, I am not surprised because I have been that person—afraid that others will notice and call me out.

Some sex-classification policies are bureaucratic in nature, while others stipulate that we be physically separated on the basis of sex. There are also sex-based "affirmative action" policies that use sex classification data to achieve a numerical balance of women and men in employment and educational institutions where one sex group has historically been absent or underrepresented.

Bureaucratic sex sorting begins even before we are born with the routine use of prenatal ultrasound technology. At twenty weeks into a pregnancy, ultrasound technicians can see whether a fetus appears to have a vagina or a penis. Based upon this information and its verification at birth, our birth certificates are marked female or male. This first sex-identity documentation becomes the basis for the subsequent sex markers that appear on our driver's licenses, state identification cards, and passports. We are asked to tick binary sex boxes on myriad bureaucratic forms ranging from school, job, mortgage, and apartment rental applications to government census forms, dental and medical intake questionnaires, online dating sites, social media and marketing surveys, and on and on.

Checking or clicking on a sex-identity box is so routinized that many of us have never questioned it. Indeed, sex classification boxes typically appear at the top of applications, signaling their importance and necessity. When my wife and I filled out the registration form for our daughter's daycare program, the first question following the space for our child's name was her sex classification. These boxes continue to appear on the papers and screens in front of us throughout our lifetimes. And sex markers stay with us until the time of our death when our death certificates describe us as having been male or female.

In addition to being bureaucratically sorted according to binary sex, we are also physically sorted into the categories of male or female, in both mandatory and voluntary ways. Are restaurants, retail stores, schools, and gyms following the law or just social custom when they build two separate rooms and label one "men" and the other "women"? Most athletic events, especially at elite levels, are segregated by binary sex. But why is this so? And should it be so, even when the competitive stakes are low or nonexistent, and differences in physical strength and skill vary so greatly intrasexually among the people we group together as boys and girls, and men and women?

Other forms of sex segregation are voluntary. For instance, in the market for higher education, prospective students have the option of applying for admission to a relatively small number of private single-sex colleges. As of this writing, there are thirty-nine women-only private colleges, and just three men-only private colleges. Why are these colleges permitted to reject students on the basis of their sex, while others are not? There are numerous associations, clubs, and programs that are "for men" or "for women," such as fraternities and sororities, so-called "gentlemen's clubs," and various sex-specific support groups. Recently, I saw a commercial for a retirement home referral service with the sex-specific name, "A Place for Mom."

Private clubs are permitted to reject members on the basis of sex, while businesses and associations that are open to the public and/or use public property such as a public park or community center can market themselves as being "for girls or women" or "for boys or men," but they are legally prohibited from turning away someone because of the person's sex. Examples of this include public gyms that cater to women, such as Lucille Roberts and Curves, and barber shops that cater to men and beauty salons that cater to women. And although "A Place for Mom" advertises exclusively toward women, the referral agency is legally obligated to help you also find a place for dad if you call and ask.

Other sex-classification policies aim to address past and ongoing sexism. These "benign" or "positive" sex discrimination policies range from temporary sex separation that seeks to provide same-sex space in which to heal, grow, and build camaraderie apart from the larger society's oppressiveness, to sex-based affirmative action programs and policies that seek to increase the presence of women or men in a particular institution. Employers have a legal responsibility to ensure that both men and women have an "equal opportunity" to apply and be considered for the jobs they post. This legal obligation extends to promotions within a company or agency.

Many job announcement advertisements include statements such as "women and minority candidates are especially encouraged to apply." Similarly, most colleges must demonstrate that both men and women have an "equal opportunity" to apply for admission. Employers and schools must collect and maintain data on the number of women and men applying for jobs and college admission, and the number of male and female applicants hired or admitted. And they must share these data with government monitoring agencies such as the Departments of Justice and Education. Organizations may want to know the sex identities of job and school applicants because they seek a more gender-diverse workforce or student body.

All of these formal sex-classification policies are supported by our strong social customs regarding how we should talk, behave, and treat others when we recognize them as being male or being female. The grammatical rules of the English language make it impossible to refer to someone in the third person without using the gendered pronouns of he or she, him or her. Pregnant people are asked by family, friends, and strangers whether they are having a boy or a girl. Some people are offended when people use the wrong gender pronoun in reference to their babies, so there are also social costs to getting sex identity "wrong." To stave off the faux pas and awkwardness that "misgendering" can elicit, some parents place headbands with bows and flowers around the bald heads of their female babies. And our gendered social norms of politeness mean that waiters and salespeople feel compelled to refer to us as "sir" and "ma'am."

Are these formal and informal sex-classification policies necessary? Are they harmful? Does gender matter?

The Argument

I believe that all of us would be better off in a society with dramatically fewer sex-classification policies. And I argue that the basic structure of antidiscrimination law can help us make this happen.

But the kind of legalism I have in mind is not adversarial. Lawsuits and the threat of lawsuits are sometimes needed in order to force people and organizations to do what they otherwise are unwilling to do. But I also believe that antidiscrimination laws can be used to inspire and bring about positive institutional change *before* conflict arises and the lawyers are called. In a series of four case studies, I show why it is in the best interests of organizations of all kinds to minimize their administration of sex. When sex classification is relevant, and it sometimes is, it is also in their best interests to redesign such policies so that the harm of sex-identity discrimination is minimized.

I suggest that organizations apply a literal and pragmatic interpretation of the diagnostic "rational relationship" test at the center of judicial review to their administrative policies regarding sex. The legal test asks whether a given policy is "rationally related" to a legitimate policy goal. In layperson's terms, this means asking whether a given sex-classification policy is harmful, and whether it is necessary.

More often than not, I find that there are better, more efficient ways for an organization to meet its policy goals than invoking sex classification. When sex is relevant to a legitimate policy goal, it behooves an organization to clearly articulate this relevance and make it transparent both to itself and to the public. Why is a sex-classification policy that was once "on the books" or customary now being eliminated? Why is a specific sex-classification policy being retained? Why is a revised or new sex-classification policy being put in place?

The Problem with "Correction"

In making this argument, I part company with the liberal strategy of the mainstream transgender civil rights movement. Their main strategy has been to assimilate and accommodate transgender individuals into existing binary sex-classification policies.

When I changed my sex identity from female to male, my employer took this approach. A series of ad hoc solutions to assimilate and accommodate me within the university's existing binary sex policies ensued. The director of human resources helped me change my name and sex markers on bureaucratic records. A single-user restroom six floors above the floor where my office is located was transformed into a unisex restroom. And I was given a key to the office in which it was located so that I could access the special restroom when it was closed. I was sent a list of all the single-user restrooms located in various buildings throughout the campus. These were few and far between. Many buildings had no such facilities. There was something amiss here, however, as I had never expressed a preference for a single-user restroom.

Assimilation is fueled by the notion of correction. But "correction" does not solve the problem that sex-classification policies cause. As long as sex-classification policies remain in place, they will always trigger discrimination. Not everyone can or wants to assimilate into prevailing gender norms. Moreover, some people's statements about their sex identities will be rejected no matter what they do or say. The details of the sex sticker case make this point abundantly clear. When Arcila used a female-marked pass, the bus operator told her that she did not look like a woman, and therefore could not use the female-marked pass she had purchased.

The appropriate correction in this case would seem to be to purchase a male-marked pass, even though she did not self-identify as male. But that sex-marked pass, too, was deemed "incorrect." The bus drivers used their own opinions about how women and men should appear and behave. And because Arcila was black, these evaluations involved judgments about how black women and black men should appear and behave. Her "wrong" gender expression could not be "corrected." She literally could not "be right." In the apt wording of transgender activist and legal scholar Dean Spade, Arcila became someone who was "administratively impossible."[22] And that made it administratively possible to take away her civil right to use the public transportation she had paid for.

My experience of being assimilated and accommodated into my workplace made me wonder how my life might have been different if the university had interpreted antidiscrimination law in a proactive and even innovative way instead of battening down its legal hatches in anticipation of a conflict. How might the institution have changed in light of my transgender experience in ways that would have benefitted other faculty, students, staff, and visitors?

What if the university had interpreted the city's gender-identity nondiscrimination law as instructing it to evaluate the harm and necessity of all its myriad sex-classification policies that ranged from the male or female boxes on its admissions and job application forms to its sex-segregated restrooms, locker rooms, sports programs, and student housing? Instead of trying to assimilate and accommodate transgender individuals into existing sex-classification policies, why not tackle the genesis of "transgender discrimination"—sex-classification, itself? Why not use transgender experience to fundamentally question the social custom of administrating sex?

But Males and Females Are Different (Aren't They?)!

There is an elephant making its way across my computer keyboard. What about the "real world" where the vast majority of people believe that there are real and important differences between girls and boys and women and men?

My argument acknowledges the existence of statistically relevant physiological, hormonal, and social differences between "males" and "females." Most people who are assigned the sex classification of male at birth have penises and testes and live their lives self-identifying and being identified by others as boys and men. Most people who are assigned the sex classification of female at birth have vaginas and ovaries and live their lives self-identifying and being identified by others as girls and women.

However, that is not true for all of the people we group together in these categories. Some people change their birth sex designation from female to male or male to female at some point or points during their lifetimes. Some people are born with physiological and/or hormonal characteristics that do not match binary Western medical definitions of dyadic sex—an experience currently referred to as intersex identity.[23] Some people identify as both male and female—an experience sometimes referred to as "gender queer" or "gender fluid." Others reject sex-identity labels, altogether, and may refer to themselves as "nonbinary" and use gender-neutral pronouns such as "they," "them," "ter," and "ze."[24]

One response to this situation is to let majoritarian sentiment determine policy making about sex. But another response is to look for ways to make both transgender and gender-nonconforming individuals and the cisgender majority better off at the same time.

Policy Redesign

I take the second approach. At the end of each case study chapter I offer pragmatic recommendations for how individuals can rethink and redesign the administration of sex in the policy venues of identity documents, restrooms, college admissions, and sports. I recommend that all organizations perform a "gender audit." This means first taking stock of all formal and informal ways that an organization invokes sex. Then, I recommend that organizations employ the legally inspired "rational relationship" test to each policy. Is the sex-classification policy harmful? Is it necessary? Could the use of sex classification be replaced by some alternative policy that is rationally and perhaps more tightly connected to specific legitimate policy goals? Each case study presents an overview of the relevant institution, a legal and political analysis of how individuals are classified according to sex by that institution, and concrete policy recommendations for eliminating or redesigning particular sex-classification policies.

Chapter Overview

Chapter 1 investigates the mandatory male or female sex markers that appear on US birth certificates, driver's licenses, and passports. Government agencies defend their use of these markers as a fraud-prevention measure. However, sex markers do not bear a rational relationship to the legitimate and important policy goal of fraud prevention. Moreover, sex markers trigger sex-identity discrimination. For these reasons, I argue that sex markers should be removed from all government-issued personal identity documents.

There are some legitimate reasons why the government would want to gather demographic sex-identity information, namely for sex-based affirmative action measures and certain public health goals. But there are more accurate ways for government agencies to gather such data such as detaching our personal identities from sex-identity data and formulating more targeted sex-related questions on surveys (e.g., the census).

Chapter 2 explores the deeply ingrained social custom of sex-segregated public restrooms. The main policy justifications for this social custom are privacy, safety, and putative sex differences in cleanliness. I find the cleanliness justification to be unsubstantiated. Privacy and safety are legitimate policy goals, but they require contextual definition and qualification. I concede that we have a reasonable expectation of some physical seclusion from others when using toilets, showers, and changing rooms, but that sex segregation is not necessary for achieving necessary physical seclusion. The problem of sex-identity discrimination can and should be solved by designing and building public restrooms in radically different ways than we currently do. I offer some ideas for how existing sex-segregated public restrooms might be renovated, and for imagining and building new no-gender bathrooms.

Chapter 3 considers the case of single-sex US colleges, and private women-only colleges in particular. The main justification for women-only private colleges is that they play a role in remediating historical and ongoing antifemale sexism in higher education. This goal is legitimate and important, but it does not require women-only admissions policies. I recommend some alternative, feminist admissions policies that are more rationally related to remedying historical sex-based disadvantage and fostering feminist education. As in the policy recommendations presented in chapter 1, these recommendations focus on formulating more accurate and useful sex-related questions on applications and other bureaucratic forms. Furthermore, it may be time to rename women's colleges "historically female colleges" in the same way that we now refer to black colleges and universities as "historically black colleges and universities."

Chapter 4 tackles the case of sex-segregated sports. Many people defend sex-segregated sports on the basis of "fair play." However, bundled up in the concept of fair play are a variety of more specific sporting goals, such as equal opportunity, gendered spectacle, student athleticism, social affinity, and fun. Sports administrators should identify the specific goals they want to achieve, along with the age of participants and the level of play (e.g., recreational, competitive, elite competitive) when they go about the task of designing transgender-inclusive sports policies that benefit all participants. As the level of competitiveness increases, sex-related physiological features, such as testosterone levels, height, and weight, become increasingly relevant. Policy makers should use these measures rather than sex classification per se to regulate athletic competition.

The conclusion and appendix look at where we can go next. I provide a how-to guide for organizations looking for ways to make their administrative practices more inclusive of people with transgender and gender-nonconforming identities. I share some of the workshop materials I use in my consulting work with organizations of various kinds and sizes. I also share the results of a gender audit that I conducted for a corporate bank so that readers may see what a gender audit looks like. In keeping with the book's main argument, the focus of the gender audit is to minimize sex-identity discrimination and boost organizational efficiency. My hope is that change makers will use it as a template for making their organizational settings better for everyone, no matter their sex identity.

1

The Sex Markers We Carry

Sex-Marked Identity Documents

Lauren Grey, a white transgender woman living in suburban Chicago, had obtained a new driver's license that showed her new name and a recent photograph that reflected her current feminine appearance. But the sex marker on her license was still male because Grey had not had the "gender reassignment" surgery that the state of Illinois required at the time in order to change the sex marker on her license from male to female. Grey, a thirty-eight-year-old graphic designer, recounted the many awkward and embarrassing questions that she was subjected to while attempting to carry out everyday public transactions. She became acutely aware of just how often the average person is asked to present a driver's license as proof of personal identity. The list ranged from getting into a bar to getting a job, renting an apartment, and navigating airport security checkpoints. When she tried to test-drive a new car, she handed over her driver's license to the salesperson. He noticed the male sex marker and began asking Grey a series of invasive questions. "They are like, 'This doesn't match.' Then you have to go into the story: 'I was born male, but now I'm not. And they are like, 'What does this mean?'"[1]

Making it possible for Grey to change the male sex marker on her driver's license to female might seem like a solution to this problem. If the sex marker on her license matched her self-definition as female, then perhaps the car salesperson would not have made her "go into the story" of being born male. The primary strategy of the mainstream transgender civil rights movement has been to make in possible for transgender people to have the sex markers on our identity documents match our felt or lived sex identity. Through lobbying and lawsuits, the movement has been very successful in bringing about this reform in the bureaucratic administration of the mandatory sex markers on passports, birth certificates, and driver's licenses.

In the wake of Grey's story being picked up by the press, Illinois joined many other states in making it easier for transgender people to change the sex markers on both their birth certificates and driver's licenses.[2] Grey has now changed the sex marker on her license to female.[3] As a gender-conforming transgender person, I have benefited from being able to change the sex markers on my identity documents to reflect my lived sex identity as male. At the same time, I recognize that this strategy of assimilation does not solve the identity document problem for all transgender people.

What Are You?

People whose appearances and voices "out" them as transgender will still have public encounters in which they are forced to explain their sex identities. And these individuals will still be vulnerable to having their statements and therefore their identity documents rejected in public transactions. This discretionary power is precisely what made the sex stickers on Philadelphia's public transit passes inherently discriminatory. It's why activists called for their removal instead of their adjustment. As previously discussed, that was the radical political meaning of Charlene Arcila's "gender identity" discrimination complaint against the Southeastern Pennsylvania Transportation Authority (SEPTA).

When she purchased and tried to use a female-marked pass, it was rejected. And when she purchased and tried to use a male-marked pass, it too was rejected. Changing the sex marker did not resolve the sex-identity discrimination that she faced. Nor did it put an end to the invasive questioning and humiliation she routinely experienced as she tried to use city buses to get around her city. When Christian A'Xavier Lovehall tried to use a female-marked transit pass as a sixteen-year-old self-described "butch lesbian" before he transitioned to male, the bus driver called him back, and asked loudly so that everyone on the bus could hear and take note, "*What* are you?"

Asking a person "*What* are you?" is very different from asking someone "*Who* are you?" The second question is relevant to the confirmation of our personal identities. The first question is not. When someone asks another person "*What* are you?" and "What do the sex stickers on your identity documents mean?" that asker is baiting the person being asked to share a story that is both awkward and humiliating. This is true even when the person being questioned has adopted sophisticated psychological coping mechanisms to mitigate and hide the hurt. Arcila's strong words were full of hurt. Amid the stares and taunts, she said, "I found myself locked in that protective zone of blackening everybody around me out of my vision."[4] Whether one is trying to board a city bus, test-drive a new car, rent an apartment, open a bank account, or buy beer, sex identity is wholly irrelevant.

The power to inspect our government-issued identity documents is the power to inspect the sex markers on these documents. In this way, sex markers offer institutional cover for administrative agents, be they police officers, car salespeople, teachers, or hospital staff, to express transgender animus. As transgender scholar-activists Paisley Currah and Dean Spade correctly point out, "the real impact of discrimination against transgender individuals is to be found in the cracks and crevices of the modern regulatory state, in the agency rules administered by particular state actors that exclude trans people" under the pretense of gender fraud.[5]

This is not to say that all or even most of the people who inspect our identity documents will use their administrative power to challenge or deny our sex-identity statements. I am optimistic enough to believe that most people do not wish to give transgender and gender-nonconforming people a hard time, or deprive us of our civil rights. Many SEPTA bus drivers chose not to hassle riders about the sex stickers on their transit passes. And I believe that there are many car salespeople, doctors, nurses, teachers, election monitors, and other administrative agents who will treat transgender and gender-nonconforming people with dignity and respect. The problem lies in the discretionary leeway that sex markers grant to administrative agents. For that leeway creates the "cracks and crevices" that we can fall into.

I argue that because the sex markers on our identity documents enable sex-identity discrimination and are not rationally related to the legitimate policy goal of personal identity verification, they should be removed. I make it sound easy. But I know that it's complicated. Sex markers have been attached to our birth certificates, driver's licenses, and passports from their inceptions. And these documents explicitly or implicitly predicate just about every other sex-classification policy that organizes US public life.

For instance, North Carolina's controversial "Bathroom Bill" is anchored by reference to the sex markers on our birth certificates. The 2016 law, also known as House Bill 2 (HB2), requires people to use the sex-segregated restroom that matches their "biological sex" in public schools and agencies throughout the state of North Carolina. The law defines biological sex as "the physical condition of being male or female, which is stated on a person's birth certificate."[6] Even when our sex-marked identity documents are not explicitly invoked, they are often implicitly invoked.

The North Carolina Republican-dominated legislature explicitly invoked birth sex designation because they believed that such evidence is implied in other sex-segregated bathroom policies across the nation. And when it comes to most sex-segregated sports, there is often an assumption that one's appearance matches the sex marker on one's identity documents. So there is no need to ask for the actual presentation of a birth certificate for proof of sex. I explore both of these policy venues (bathrooms and sports) in the chapters ahead.

The Meaning of Sex and Gender

The government agencies that issue and administrate our sex-marked birth certificates, driver's licenses, and passports never define the terms "sex" and "gender." The wording of recently adopted instructions for how transgender people can "correct" the sex markers on these documents offers some clues as to what various government agencies mean by "sex" and "gender." However, these ad hoc sex-marker-amendment policies falsely imply that the original decision to include sex markers on our identity documents "goes without saying," and need not be explained. It is ironic that socially and bureaucratically important concepts such as sex and gender are so poorly defined by the agencies that use them.

Gender theory scholars, by contrast, have had a lot to say about the terms "sex" and "gender." When I began teaching courses on feminist political theory in the early 1990s, I followed the feminist pedagogical norm at the time of drawing a distinction between the terms on the first day of classes. I taught my students, just as I had been taught, that "sex" referred to the biological categories of female and male, and that "gender" referred to the socially constructed norms that we, as a society, construct and attach to the sex categories of male and female. Primary physiological sex differences such as genitalia and reproductive organs, along with secondary biological characteristics such as muscularity, fat distribution, breasts, body and facial hair, and tone of voice, were the telltale, "obvious" markers of being a male or being a female.

Gender norms concerning masculinity and femininity were socially constructed, and not born into our bodies. Most liberal feminist theory and jurisprudence focuses on changing specific normative gender stereotypes of masculinity and femininity, namely those stereotypes that are used to deprive someone of equal opportunities because she *is* female, or because he *is* male.[7] The assumption in this formulation is that the "biological" sex categories of maleness and femaleness that anchor gender stereotypes are *immutable* personal characteristics that we are born with and cannot alter. Some radical feminists argue that gender socialization is so strong that we experience the "demands of femininity" and masculinity as the very definition of what it means to be a woman and what it means to be a man.[8] The implication here is that socially constructed sex categories are immutable because they are drilled into us by parenting and socialization to the point that we cannot personally change them.[9]

But historians of science and postmodern gender theorists challenged this assumption about the immutability of biological sex in the 1990s. They argued that the categories of male and female are not, in fact, as stable as conventional feminist wisdom had believed. Medical and psychological discourses were steeped in stereotypes of female inferiority, and these prejudices were interlaced with racism, classism, and heterosexism. Historians of science such as Anne Fausto-Sterling and Thomas Lacqueur exposed the masculine-biased frameworks used by scientists and physicians to "determine" and "fix" misogynistic renderings of female sex identity.[10] Think for example about how clitorises and labia are often described as variations of penises and scrotums, instead of the other way around.

Feminist psychoanalytic theorists highlighted the misogyny in the works of Sigmund Freud and other patriarchs of Western psychology who used terms such as "hysteria" to describe female but not male patients with the same symptoms.[11] Western medical discourse produced the notion of binary sexual difference and hierarchy out of a world of physiological and endocrinal sexual variation. Critical race feminists such as Dorothy Roberts highlighted the intersectional racist-sexist dimensions of these authoritative descriptions of maleness and femaleness.[12]

Postmodern theorists deepened this critique of medical sex by giving a fuller account of how contemporary conceptions of sex and gender are mutually constructed by seemingly discrete discursive institutions, such as law, science, and popular culture. Gender theorist Judith Butler introduced the term "sex/gender" to indicate this mutuality and the term "performance" to theorize how our ideas of sex/gender are produced and reproduced. Butler rejected the liberal presumption that we have or possess sex/gender identities, and theorized instead that each of us *does* or *performs* sex/gender in our actions—how we dress, speak, and otherwise behave.[13]

The verb "perform" connotes the role of repetition in generating and sustaining social norms that create such momentum in our day-to-day lives that we often mistake them for something a priori to human experience, something "natural" or "God-given" that exists outside of history and beyond our personal control. The fact that sex/gender norms are subject to historical and cultural change reveals the constructed nature of our sex/gender performances. At the same time, the repetitive and compulsive nature of our sex/gender performances means that sex/gender norms are deeply ingrained and highly regulated social customs that we experience *as if* they were unchangeable. Postmodern gender theory has shed important light on the fact that when we speak of sex we implicitly speak of gender norms, and vice versa.

The problem with collapsing the terms "sex" and "gender," however, is that doing so robs us of a language with which to differentiate between the sexism of sex-based disadvantage and the sexism of sex-identity discrimination triggered by sex-classification policies. Most of our social practice has not absorbed Fausto-Sterling's or Butler's claims. Indeed, even many of us who teach and write about these interventions do not consistently use them to alter our self-conceptions and perceptions of others. This is evident in a great deal of feminist research and teaching, where transgender and intersex experience is still often explained as exceptional, instead of being used to fundamentally challenge the idea that the terms "man" and "woman" imply particular body parts.[14]

Sex discrimination jurisprudence has exacerbated this problem by using the terms "sex" and "gender" interchangeably as synonyms without acknowledging the constructed nature of our sexed bodies, and our basic right to say who we are in relation to the categories of male and female.[15] Just because we perform sex/gender simultaneously, and both are socially constructed, does not eviscerate the conceptual distinction between sex and gender. Gender stereotypes are at the heart of traditional sexism, which focuses on sex-based disadvantage, or "artificial constraints" on a person's opportunities "because of sex."[16] Sex-identity sexism envelops traditional sexism, but goes further to assess who is permitted to be in the categories of male and female.

Birth Certificates

The first sex-marked identity document that we acquire is a birth certificate. All people who are born in the United States are issued birth certificates by the state or territory in which they are born, and every state and territory requires that the birth certificates they issue include a "male" or "female" sex designation. When prenatal development is monitored via ultrasound, a medical technician determines the baby's sex identity prior to birth. At twenty weeks into a pregnancy, a penis or vagina is typically visible on the ultrasound monitor. Parents are given the option of learning this information, or waiting to hear "It's a boy!" or "It's a girl!" at the moment of birth. The delivering physician makes that announcement based upon a quick visual inspection of the baby's genitalia.

When a baby is born in a hospital, a sex marker of male or female is entered into a birth certificate application form, which is then passed along to the "mother" to complete. "She" is asked to fill in additional information about herself and the baby's "father." I use quotation marks here because not all delivering parents self-identify as "mothers," and not all second parents self-identify as "fathers." Some transgender men with ovaries and uteruses can and do become pregnant, and some transgender women whose bodies produce sperm can sire children. In order to be more institutionally efficient, hospitals might consider using the terms "delivering parent" and "second parent" to more accurately retrieve the information they are seeking: *who* the child's legal parents are, not *what* their sex identities are.

There is precedent for this degendering of parents in the US State Department's 2010 decision to replace the terms "mother" and "father" with "Parent 1" and "Parent 2" on its passport application forms. In making this administrative change, the State Department sought to "recognize different types of families."[17] Cisgender (a term used to refer to non-transgender people) parents are not harmed by this more inclusive and institutionally efficient format because they retain their identities as "parents."

When a baby is born outside of a hospital, parents are legally required to register the child's birth with the state, usually within ten days. In such cases, parents are responsible for indicating the sex of their child on an out-of-hospital state-issued birth worksheet.[18]

This seems like a simple declaration for a physician, midwife, or parent to make. However, medical experts report that one child in somewhere between fifteen hundred and two thousand births has "noticeably atypical" genitalia.

And many more people are born with subtler sex anatomy variations, some of which become noticeable only later in their lifetimes.[19] People who are born with chromosomal, physiological, and/or endocrinal features that do not neatly correspond to our culturally determined definitions of dyadic sex are described as "intersex." Some intersex conditions, such as aphallia, whereby a "genetic" male with XY chromosomes is born without a penis, are apparent at birth. Other conditions may not be apparent or "diagnosed" until puberty or even later, such as androgen insensitivity syndrome (AIS), whereby a person is born with XY chromosomes but the person's cells cannot absorb "male hormones" or androgens. People with AIS appear to be and mostly self-identify as female, but do not menstruate, lack a cervix, and have sparse underarm and pubic hair.[20]

Since the mid-twentieth century, the medical protocol has been to perform surgeries on infants diagnosed with intersex conditions in order to "fix" their atypical bodies. The protocol focuses on surgical intervention during the first eighteen months of a child's life based upon the belief that "gender identity" is malleable during that period. In her canonical gender theory essay, "How to Build a Man," Fausto-

Sterling demonstrates that the medical "fixing" of intersex bodies has been skewed in favor of creating "normal" boys more so than "normal" girls. Most corrective surgeries have been to transform micro penises into vaginas.[21]

In the 1990s, many adults who had been surgically "fixed" as babies began sharing anguished experiences of having been forced by their parents under doctors' orders to take on a sex identity that conflicted with their own felt sex identity.[22] Hence, a major political demand of intersex activism has been to end these early childhood surgical interventions so that individuals can make their own decisions about their sex identities later in life.[23]

The Intersex Society of North America (ISNA) foregrounds this right to sex-identity self-authority in their mission statement, which reads, "The ISNA is devoted to systemic change to end shame, secrecy, and unwanted genital surgeries for people born with anatomy that *someone decided* is not standard for male or female."[24] And while it is true that most people are not born with intersex conditions, the politics of "fixing sex" affects all of us. As Katrina Karkazis puts it, "the frequency of intersexuality is less important than ideas about how to make these infants 'normal' boys or girls." She poses a poignant question, "What bodily parts, experiences, and capabilities are necessary for an individual to *feel* he or she is a man or a woman?"[25] And is sex identity something that can or should *ever* be administratively determined for us by others at birth?

The government has its own reasons for sorting us according to sex. Birth certificates enable the government to "see" us in certain ways in order for it to carry out its administrative objectives.[26] Our birth certificates are considered vital government records, and are kept as permanent records in the Department of Vital Statistics in the state where we are born. In addition to live births, states also collect and keep "vital statistics" regarding marriage, divorce, and fetal deaths. Certificates of live births became "vital" to government agencies and individual Americans with the advent of government welfare programs that required proof of a beneficiary's existence as a fraud-prevention measure.[27] In 2008, 97 percent of Americans had birth certificates.[28]

These identity documents have become administratively normalized within the public sphere as proof not just of our existence, our "live birth," but also of our age. Hence, parents need to present their children's birth certificates when they register them for school. State-collected birth records also inform the federal government of when we reach the age of sixty-five, and become eligible for social security payments and Medicare. The sex marker on our birth certificates is not "vital" or even relevant to these objectives.

Driver's Licenses

To obtain a driver's license you must present your birth certificate. Like the collection and maintenance of vital records, the licensing of drivers also falls under the residual constitutional power of individual states.[29] It is both a major source of state revenue and a way of standardizing safe driving practices. The dramatic increase in the number of American drivers in the post–World War II era made it possible for the driver's license to become a common proof of personal identity in a wide range of administrative venues.[30] Recall Lauren Grey's description of the difficulty that her male-marked driver's license caused in everyday transactions. We are asked for ID when we seek employment, register to vote, apply for insurance, open a bank account, apply for a home mortgage, rent an apartment, receive medical care, and sign mobile phone service contracts, and the list goes on. Police officers inspect our driver's licenses in all traffic stops.

Driver's licenses have become the standard means of enforcing state-mandated minimum age requirements for purchasing alcohol and tobacco products. Birth certificates and passports are generally accepted alternatives to driver's licenses for age verification, but very few people carry their birth certificate or passport with them while going about their everyday public-sphere activities.[31] Indeed, driver's licenses are so frequently demanded as proof of personal identification and age that most states have created analogous state identification cards for nondrivers. I cannot think of an administrative setting where a driver's license or state identification card is officially required as proof of whether someone is male or female.

The federal government has intervened to regulate the information that appears on all state-issued driver's licenses. In 2005, the US Congress passed the REAL ID Act, a law aimed at standardizing the identity-verification features on driver's licenses and state identity cards. The official purpose of the REAL ID Act is to enhance homeland security in the wake of the 9/11 attacks. Its more specific genesis can be traced to an official advisory issued by the US Department of Homeland Security warning that "male [suicide] bombers may dress as females in order to discourage scrutiny."

Title II of the act, "Improved Security for Drivers' Licenses and Personal Identification Cards," mandates that all states include the following information on driver's licenses and state identification cards: the licensed person's full legal name, date of birth, and *gender*, the license or identification number, a digital photograph of the person, the person's principal residency address and signature, physical security features to "prevent tampering, counterfeiting, or duplication of the document for fraudulent purposes," as well as a common machine-readable technology such as a magnetic strip. The REAL ID Act also requires states to subject all digital identification photos to facial image capture technology and that no license or identification card be valid for more than eight years.[32] All driver's licenses use the term "sex," whereas the REAL ID Act uses the term "gender." Neither law defines these terms.

Passports

Passports document a person's national identity and are required for crossing international borders. Like birth certificates and driver's licenses, passports are also a relatively recent historical development. They were introduced following World War I. All American citizens, whether born or naturalized in the United States, are eligible for a US passport, and must apply to the US State Department for their passports. The State Department requires all passports bear a male or female sex marker. Although more Americans travel internationally these days than at any other time in history, only 25 percent of Americans currently hold a passport, compared to 97 percent who have birth certificates.[33] To apply for a new passport a citizen must take the following documents in person to a passport-acceptance facility such as a courthouse, post office, public library, or designated county or municipal office: a two-by-two-inch color photograph, a birth certificate, and a valid government-issued identity document such as a driver's license or state or tribal identification card.[34]

Race-Marked Identity Documents

The story of race markers and government-issued identity documents has been very different from that of sex markers. Up until the black civil rights movement gained momentum in the 1960s, race markers were standard features of most US birth certificates and driver's licenses. Civil rights organizations lobbied to have race markers removed from birth certificates and driver's licenses. Some of this pressure involved lawsuits, and some states and localities changed their race marker policies without legal pressure.

In 1962, the president of the American Statistician Society described the case against race markers in the following way: "1) the position that the collection of such information violates a person's privacy if not his constitutional and legal rights and constitutes an affront to his dignity; 2) the fear that such information may be used to deal with the person or group in a categoric way, and thus evoke discriminatory practices."[35] In 1961, New York became the first city to eliminate race markers from birth certificates.[36]

Getting rid of race markers on these documents solved one problem but created another. Without racial markers on identity documents, it was difficult and sometimes impossible to collect data on when and where racial discrimination was occurring. The problem came to a head in the debates over race-based affirmative action that began during the 1970s and continue today. Supporters of these "benign" or "positive" forms of racial discrimination drew attention to racial classification as a way to "affirmatively" address invidious racial discrimination. Some people argue that race markers should be reinstated on driver's licenses as a way to collect data about racial profiling by police officers in making traffic stops.[37]

The federal Centers for Disease Control and Prevention (CDC) also has a vested interest in collecting race and sex data to track and measure public health trends. The CDC issued its most recent recommendation of standard birth certificate data collection in 2003. The form given to parents (usually the "mother") asks for the self-reported racial classification of the mother and father. But the CDC does not specify how it will use such data to record the racial classification of the child.[38] This raises the question about what definition of racial identity is being used. Is it the self-reported first-person notion of racial identity, or a third-person perspective of how we are perceived by others?

These two perspectives can yield different results. For example, my birth mother was white and my birth father African American. I identify as either biracial or black depending on the context in which I'm asked. How others perceive my race varies and depends on context. I've been welcomed or ushered into just about every brown ethnic group at one time or another. There is a compelling case to be made that it is third-person racial perception that matters most in the collection of racial data that are to be used to track and measure racial discrimination. However, this directive has not made its way onto the various bureaucratic forms that ask us to check one or more racial boxes.

The failure to explain why race markers were removed, as well as why we are being asked to check racial boxes on various forms, is a major problem. The use of race in government policies receives the highest level of scrutiny by courts because historically race has been used to deprive racial minorities of their civil rights.[39] In legalese, this means that when the government invokes race it must show that its use of racial classification is "narrowly tailored" to meet a "legitimate" and "compelling" goal. In other words, the government must show that the policy goal in question is extremely important and necessary, and there are no ways to meet the compelling goal without invoking race. This is known as a "strict scrutiny" test, and it is the reason that race markers and questions have been removed from many bureaucratic forms.

When racial classification questions do show up on forms, there is typically a note stating that divulging this information is voluntary. It would be helpful if the designers of such forms included an explanation of *why* the question is voluntary, why such a question is being asked, and what definition of race is being used. But courts have not forced or even instructed policy makers to include such information on the forms they use.

When I argue for the elimination of particular sex-classification policies and the redesign of others, I strongly recommend that policy makers explain *why* sex markers are being removed. When sex is preserved as part of a policy, I urge policy makers to explain what definition of sex is being used, and to what end. When it comes to sex classification, courts have adopted an "intermediate" level of scrutiny that falls somewhere between the lowest (rational relationship test) and highest (strict scrutiny) levels of scrutiny. The argument for this "intermediate scrutiny" is grounded in the government's historical record of sex discrimination. In the past, the government has sometimes used sex classification for discriminatory purposes, but not always, and less so than in the case of racial classification. Under intermediate scrutiny, government and state actors must prove that the use of sex classification bears a "substantial relationship" to a goal that is not just legitimate but also "important."[40] Courts grant the most deference to government policies involving other classifications. In cases of, for instance, age or geographical location, the "rational relationship test" is used.

Failing the Rational Relationship Test

I would argue that the use of sex markers on government-issued identity documents fails even the lowest level of judicial scrutiny. If I am right about that, then this bureaucratic use of sex certainly fails to meet the higher standard of "intermediate" judicial scrutiny that courts apply to cases involving sex. Government agencies have a legitimate and important interest in keeping track of our personal identities for purposes such as taxation, law enforcement, and public health. Correspondingly, we have a personal interest in having our personal identities verified in many of the transactions we make in the public sphere to reduce our exposure to the crime of identity theft, which can drain our financial assets, damage our credit scores, and wreak emotional havoc on our lives.

However, sex markers are not helpful in guarding against personal identity fraud because maleness and femaleness are characteristics that we share with many other people. The inadequacy of sex verification as fraud protection is spoofed in the 2013 Hollywood comedy *Identity Thief*, in which a female con artist named Diana, played by Melissa Mc-Carthy, steals a man named Sandy's credit card information and social security number, and goes on a spending spree. Sandy, played by Jason Bateman, soon discovers that in addition to not being able to use his credit cards to buy things such as gas, he also has a court summons for crimes committed by Diana in his name in another state. The movie highlights another reason why sex markers are poor proxies for verifying personal identity: the fact that many people have gender-neutral or "unisex" names, Sandy being just one of many examples. Moreover, most identity theft is done online or by telephone, where sex identity is easy enough to fake.

Why Sex Identity "Correction" Doesn't Solve the Problem

As I mentioned earlier, the mainstream transgender civil rights strategy has focused on making it possible and easier for people to change the sex markers on their birth certificates, driver's licenses, and passports in order to reflect their current or "lived" sex identity.[41] This liberal correction has taken two forms: assimilation and accommodation. Both strategies appear to be a step in the right direction because they acknowledge that sex identity is a mutable characteristic that is personally changeable. However, neither assimilation nor accommodation solves the problem of sex-identity discrimination because they leave intact the source of sex-identity discrimination: bureaucratic sex classification itself.

Correction is also problematic insofar as it implies a "mistake" that may or may not correspond to a particular person's self-understanding of sex-identity change. In his beautifully written memoir, Aaron Raz Link, a white self-described female-to-male transsexual, historian of science, and professional clown, challenges the persistent stereotype that transgender people are "trapped in the wrong body," and acquire a "new body" via sex-identity transition. He begins his story of his sex change by locating himself within a broader human story of the inevitable mutability of all human bodies over time, and the common struggle to find one's sense of belonging in the places we inhabit. There are ways in which he is normal, and ways in which he is not.

In an early chapter titled "ABC," Raz reaches for connection before embarking upon his story of difference:

> This body has changed since I was born. It will change before I leave it, in ways I can't anticipate. How do any of us recognize ourselves, given the changes we go through between birth and death? Depending on your point of view, trapped within this question are answers about autoimmune disease, calls from God, cancer, pregnancy, schizophrenia, samsara, transsexualism. Like everyone else, I have had the same body since the

day I was born. Approximately every seven years, most of my cells, like yours, have been replaced by new cells. I am trapped within my body as little and as much as every other human being. To believe otherwise, is to deny a miracle; I have changed and there is only one of me.[42]

Raz does not claim to speak for all transgender and gender-nonconforming people. A liberal model of correction may resonate for some or even many transgender and gender-nonconforming people. However, there are other people, such as Raz, for whom this paradigm does not ring true.

The paradigm of correction forces bureaucracies into some linguistic knots. All states have policies that allow for individuals to submit applications to correct mistakes on their birth certificates and driver's licenses. So, when a state has subsequently adopted a bureaucratic procedure for transgender individuals to change their sex markers on these documents, it has differentiated between these two kinds of correction. California, for instance, distinguishes between "gender reassignment" and a "gender error" in its administrative guidelines for changing its birth certificate sex markers. "'Gender *reassignment*' is when a person has undergone clinically appropriate treatment for the purpose of gender transition. This is not the same as 'gender *error*,' which is when a person's sex is *incorrectly stated* on the original birth certificate by the person preparing the birth certificate and registering the birth."[43] Here, the state of California ruminates on the reasons for a sex marker change request. Requesting to change a sex marker due to a clerical error falls into one administrative category. In this category, the person's sex identity has not changed. It was simply recorded incorrectly. In the second case, the person's sex identity has changed, and the sex marker change is meant to reflect that change. But I wonder, does the state have a legitimate interest in differentiating between these two scenarios?

And more pointedly, does the government have a legitimate interest in knowing the details of my or anyone's sex-identity changes? Transgender studies scholars Paisley Currah and Lisa Jean Moore trace the history of how New York lawmakers framed the "public interest" in regulating sex marker changes to its birth certificates. The paper trail between 1965 and 2006 shows a shift from a concern about fraud to one of permanence. Early on, the state emphasized that "'for the protection of the general public, [one's status as a transsexual] should be known.'"[44] The evidence shows that the main concern was to protect "straight" men from being duped into marrying a transsexual woman. "One doctor cited the case of 'a man who marries one of these persons with the expectation of having a family.'"[45] There is no mention in these historical discussions about female-to-male transsexuals.

Later, the state shifts to focus on its vested interest in ensuring that petitions to change birth sex markers be "permanent." Permanence meant irreversible surgery to demonstrate the person's commitment to "their new gender role."[46] New York State abandoned its surgical requirement in 2014, as have many other states. However, the new policy retains the paradigm of permanence by requiring a notarized affidavit from a physician or a physician's assistant to accompany all applications for birth certificate "correction."[47]

Britain's "Gender Recognition Act," enacted in 2004, explicitly invokes permanent assimilation as the legal standard of transgender recognition. It allows "transsexual people who have taken decisive steps to live fully and *permanently* in their acquired gender" to be legally recognized in their "preferred gender role."[48] With this framing, the British government limits the legal sanctioning of sex-identity transition to those who are able to demonstrate permanent assimilation into maleness or femaleness.

The paradigm of permanence is strongly implied in most US laws by the requirement that individuals' decision to change their sex marker on an official identity document be medically authorized. But the requirements for medical authorization vary across agencies and levels of government. Why must our understanding of sex-identity change be limited to a single event of permanent assimilation into the opposite binary sex category? And what does it mean to live "fully" in one's "acquired gender"? The language of acquisition is problematic, too, as the connotation that one's lived or felt sex identity is not intrinsic may resonate with some, but not all transgender and gender-nonconforming people.

While the federal government has mandated that sex markers appear on all driver's licenses and state identification cards, it has not issued any standards or guidelines for how states should handle requests by individuals to alter the sex markers on their driver's licenses. In this void, states have developed and adjusted their own administrative procedures concerning sex-marker changes. Some states require the presentation of a court order stating that the person has "legally" transitioned from male to female or female to male. Others require the presentation of the person's birth certificate that has been officially amended. The vast majority of states require some sort of confirmation from a medical provider that the person is "transgender."

The deference to medical authority here is asserted rather than explained. So even those who argue that sex amendment rules should be adjusted to meet advancing medical knowledge regarding sex-identity change are misguided because they fail to question the turn to medical expertise in the first place.[49]

The policy reform of allowing transgender people to "correct" the sex markers on our identity documents also doesn't guarantee its enforcement. For example, the state of Kansas has a policy that explicitly allows transgender people to change the sex markers on their birth certificates. However, the state agency responsible for processing these applications stopped processing them shortly after Governor Sam Brownback took office in 2012. Stephanie Mott, a fifty-eight-year-old transgender woman, is suing the state for failing to carry out the very policy it enacted. In her words, "It's so important for me that my birth certificate reflect my authentic self. Having accurate identity documents is not only a matter of human dignity but also an issue of safety. I shouldn't have to out myself as transgender every time I apply for a job or when I register to vote."[50]

And even when a person adheres to the law and obtains the proper documentation from a medical provider, sex-identity discrimination can and does still occur in the administration of such requests. In 2014, a California DMV worker harassed and publicly humiliated a transgender woman after she handed him her properly documented sex-marker amendment form. "When she presented her paperwork to the clerk, the DMV employee was friendly until discovering that she was transgender. At that point he became visibly angry and began to loudly lecture her on the 'sin' of being transgender, calling Ms. Doe 'the devil,' until she broke down crying. A manager later apologized and told Ms. Doe that the employee had 'done this before.'" She filed a lawsuit alleging gender identity discrimination and violation of her privacy rights. California settled the case out of court.[51] One response to this administrative sex-identity discrimination is to institute educational trainings, and for DMV managers to do a better job of supervising the clerks they manage. But a far more effective way of eliminating such discrimination is to remove all sex markers from driver's licenses, thereby obviating the state's participation in administrating sex identity altogether.

The State Department revised its policy for changing passport sex markers in 2010, and made further changes in 2011. Previously, a person had to submit a "data correction form," along with documentation from a physician stating that the person had undergone "sex reassignment surgery." The revised policy eliminates the surgical requirement, and replaces it with a less specific appeal to medical authority. If the applicant is submitting other identification documents that do not bear an updated "correct" sex marker, then the applicant must submit a letter from a physician attesting that the person "has had appropriate clinical treatment for gender transition."[52]

The wording of this administrative law is too vague to offer any clear guidance. It puts medical providers in the position of using their own subjective definitions of "appropriate clinical treatment." Some providers will be willing to write supportive letters, but others will be unwilling. This puts transgender and gender-nonconforming individuals in the precarious position of having to seek out and rely upon a particular provider's individual discretion, which means being subject and captive to a particular provider's sex-identity assessment, be it negative, positive, or neutral.

Why More Sex Categories Won't Solve the Problem

Another approach that fails to address the full scope of the sex-identity discrimination caused by sex-marked identity documents is the addition of more sex-identity categories. The United States has not adopted this accommodation approach, but some other countries have. In 2013, Australia passed legislation that added a third sex marker option of "X," in addition to "M" or "F," to its passports. According to the law, X represents the sex category of "indeterminate," and is available only to Australians who were born with intersex conditions, and transgender Australians who can produce a "letter of support" from a physician.[53] Bangladesh added a similar third sex marker option of "other" to its passports in 2013, and India passed legislation in 2005 that added a third sex marker option of "E," which stands for eunuch. In 2013, Germany gave intersex adults, but not transgender adults, the third option of "X" on both their passports and birth certificates. Germany's law also gives the parents of intersex infants the option of leaving the sex designation on their children's birth certificate blank.[54]

Adding more sex markers is problematic because the practice neither dismantles nor significantly challenges the bureaucratic use of the traditional sex binary. Even efforts to extend government sex classification policies to include people who reject the binary terms "man" or "woman" end up reinforcing the sex binary by leaving it intact. These policies create exceptional categories. Some transgender, intersex, and gender-nonconforming people may embrace a third sex marker option, but others may feel stigmatized by such additive accommodation. In the next chapter, I show how this additive third "separate but equal" approach also fails to alleviate the sex discrimination caused by sex-segregated public restrooms.

One might defend these reforms on the basis that they acknowledge sex identity as personally changeable and not always dyadic. This could be helpful in terms of educating the broader public about the existence of transgender and intersex people. If this became a bureaucratic norm, then administrative agents would come to expect that some people's identity documents would have a third sex-identity marker. This might have changed the negative interactions that Grey had at the car dealership. But that would hinge on greater cultural and societal acceptance of transgender lives. In my opinion, the removal of sex markers from these documents would help to bring about substantial cultural reform, as it would send a strong message to all of us that a person's sex classification is irrelevant to most public transactions.

But . . . Males and Females Are Different (Aren't They?)!

When sex-identity discrimination is not a predictable part of your everyday life in public settings, when there is no awkward story about your sex identity to go into with a stranger checking your birth certificate, driver's license, or passport, it is easy to dismiss the problem of sex-marked identity documents as insignificant. After all, most people's appearances match the sex markers on their identity documents.

The gender theorist Jack Halberstam deepens this truism by pointing out that "the very flexibility and elasticity of the terms 'man' and 'woman' ensures their durability. To test this proposition, look around any public space and notice how few present formulaic versions of gender and yet how few are unreadable or totally ambiguous."[55] Many women fall short of feminine ideals and are still recognizable as women, and many men fall short of masculine ideals and are still recognizable as men.

The durable elasticity of binary sex categories tells us that sex-identity discrimination entails something else in addition to the sex-role stereotyping that generates sex-based disadvantage. Sex-identity discrimination involves the judgment that a person has stretched the elastic bands of binary sex "too far," to the point of breaking free of one sex category and trying to join its opposite. And when people look like this is what they are "trying" to do, they often end up in the "no-man, no-woman's land" where Charlene Arcila found herself as both her female-marked and male-marked transit passes were rejected by the bus drivers inspecting them and her.

People who are readable as women or men are generally not asked to produce documentation of their sex identity, even when sex identity is directly relevant to a benefit as important as sex-based affirmative action or as trivial as a ladies' night drink special. The ski resort I used to frequent in the Poconos had a "men's Monday" discount that I happily took advantage of following my sex-identity transition to male, because, well, why not? But I was never asked to hand over my driver's license for proof of my eligibility.

Had I been asked to do so, the sex marker on my driver's license would have substantiated my claiming of the discount because I had gone through the process of changing the sex marker and name on my driver's license. But had I requested the "men's Monday" discounted lift ticket two years earlier, when I appeared to the world as a masculine woman, there is a good chance that my license would have been inspected. There is also a good chance that it would not have been. It would have been up to the discretion of the person selling me the ticket. And that is precisely the problem.

Should the Government Ever Use Sex Classification?

Do government agencies have a "compelling" or even "rational" interest in collecting and recording sex-identity information about us, at all? I can think of two legitimate reasons for such data collection: the administration of sex-specific policies such as male-only military conscription, and the administration of sex-based affirmative action policies that aim to remediate historical and ongoing sexism. Now that women are fully integrated into the armed forces, I see no reason not to include them in conscription. Another option would be to eliminate the draft, as an all-volunteer military has been our norm since the Vietnam War. The legalization of same-sex marriage obviates the need to use the terms "wife" and "husband" in government-run benefits policies.

When it comes to sex-based affirmative action, I agree with philosopher Laurie Shrage that "the state only needs to track a person's lived sex, which can be verified by each individual."[56] Employers wishing to recruit and retain female employees are justifiably interested in knowing people's current sex identity, not the sex identity they were assigned at birth based upon genital inspection. Indeed, unless a person's genitals are directly relevant to a given job description (a bona fide occupational qualification [BFOQ] in legalese), as in certain kinds of sex work such as pornography, then the disclosure of such information is irrelevant to hiring and promotion, and a violation of our right to privacy.

Some people argue that transgender women who transition to female as adults should not benefit from sex-based affirmative action because they did not experience the sexism that comes along with being raised and socialized as female.[57] This is one interpretation of sex-based affirmative action: remediation of the sexism personally experienced by individuals. But such policies can also be more present- and future-oriented, and focus on the current representation of girls and women, as a group, in a given organization or institution. In that case, a transgender woman would qualify for sex-based affirmative action aimed at increasing the number of women in a school or job. And by the same logic, I would not qualify for such affirmative action at this point in my life even though I lived for thirty-eight years as a female. These are important questions for organizations and institutions to grapple with and explicitly articulate as they design their recruitment, retention, and administrative policies.

Are there legitimate and compelling scientific and medical reasons for the government to collect and maintain sex-identity information about us? A government agency such as the CDC has legitimate public health reasons for collecting and maintaining sex-specific data. How-ever, the agency should define its use of these terms and clearly articulate the "substantial" connection between its use of sex classification and its institutional objectives. Instead of using "female" or "male" as a proxy for particular body parts, the agency may find that the more targeted language of "people with uteruses" or "people with prostate glands" is more statistically inclusive.

At the same time, the creators of these questions should take into account the fact that some transgender men and women use different terms to describe their genitals. For instance, some transgender men and gender-nonconforming cisgender women refer to their clitorises as penises, and some do not, or use some other terminology. Some transgender women and gender-nonconforming cisgender men refer to their penises as clitorises, or use some other terminology.[58] This may sound like heavy-handed political correctness that goes "too far." But what we are really talking about here is gathering and maintaining *accurate* medical data. When it comes to provision of individual health care, this direct descriptive wording is even more critical, as health care providers are looking for individualized information about us in the context of aggregate data about people "like us" (e.g., people with ovaries, uteruses, and cervixes, and people with testicles and prostate glands).

When it comes to birth certificates, one might argue that state governments should at least be permitted to collect aggregate data concerning the number of live female and male births for demographic purposes. I would argue, however, that the decennial census conducted by the federal government is a much better way of capturing demographic sex-identity data because it is a voluntary questionnaire that recurs every ten years. Of course, it is highly unlikely that Census Bureau policymakers were taking into account the mutability of sex identity when they added "gender" questions to the decennial census. But now that the question is there, the federal government has a plum opportunity to clearly explain to respondents what definition of sex or gender they are being asked to voluntarily disclose and why. The racial identity questions on the census have been contested and changed over time.[59] The time has come for the government to critically assess its use of sex classification on the census.

Policy Redesign

I recommend that relevant agencies remove sex markers from the identity documents they issue. At the same time, government agencies have some legitimate and compelling reasons for retaining certain sex-identity data, such as affirmative action monitoring. In doing so, they should clearly identify what kind of sex-identity data they are gathering, and they should detach our personal identities from such data. For instance, states collecting live-birth sex-identity data should formally acknowledge that such data are based on genital inspection at birth. There should be an acknowledgment that our sex identity might change later in life. When we apply for driver's licenses and passports, the issuing agencies might ask us for our current sex identity, and make the provision of the self-reported data voluntary.

Given that sex-identity markers are poor proxies for personal identification, government agencies should focus on techniques that are in fact "rationally related" to the legitimate government goal of preventing personal identity fraud. Advancements in biometrics (measurable human characteristics) are promising and already being used in the private sector and some government agencies for identity verification. To function as a personal identity-verification characteristic, a general trait must be universally held, invariable over time, and unique to individuals. Some examples are fingerprints, palm veins, iris and face shape, hand geometry, and DNA. Biometric techniques are promising because they zero in on unique personal identity features that are (mostly) immutable, instead of sex identity, which is mutable and not a unique personal characteristic. The REAL ID Act moves in this direction when it calls for all states to include face recognition technology on all driver's licenses and state identity cards.

The use of biometrics is not without its critics. There is reason to be cautious about using technology to locate and "pin down" our personal identities in our bodies. Concerns over the loss of privacy and liberty that increased governmental surveillance can produce are valid.[60] As Jonathan Finn points out, facial recognition technology is based upon the historical assertion that there are distinct races that are inherently and objectively distinguishable.[61] Finding personal identity in the body also presumes a certain kind of able body. For example, not everybody has fingerprints or irises.

Non-body-based methods of verifying personal identity include asking us security questions that only we are likely to know, such as the last four digits of our social security number, our birth date and the name of the hospital in which we were born, our mother's maiden name, and the name of our first employer. To strengthen this approach to personal identity verification, experts recommend that we provide false answers to some of these questions that effectively bury the answers further within our own minds. There are drawbacks, of course, to burying the keys to our personal identities in our memories. It can be hard to recall the false answers that we gave to the questions meant to elicit our personal information because the information is false! Individual organizations and institutions will need to figure out which specific combination of body- and mind-based personal identity verification best serves their particular goals.

Removing sex markers from government-issued identity documents is a small but powerful way for government agencies to realign their administrative goals and policies. Everyone in the relevant "universe" benefits, and no one is disadvantaged. Sex-classification-amendment paperwork and the associated cost, which is significant, would dissolve. Currently agencies must devise sex-marker-amendment policies and expend labor processing applications and fielding questions. Although our government has some legitimate reasons for collecting sex-classification information about us in aggregate, it has no business collecting and keeping information about our personal sex-identity decisions.

Conclusion

Eradicating sex markers from our birth certificates, passports, driver's licenses, and state identity cards will not completely uproot sex-identity discrimination and oppression. However, it is an important step that would have profound ripple effects across a wide range of administrative policy venues where these documents are requested and demanded. In the chapters to come, I investigate long-standing administrative customs of sex-segregated public restrooms, single-sex colleges, and sports.

Government-issued identity documents are relevant to the administration of such policies because they "document" and stand as written, physical proof of what is often presumed to be our "legal" and "biological" sex. I have shown in this chapter that such legal documentation is built upon a presumption that crumbles under even the lowest level of judicial scrutiny, let alone the heightened level of "intermediate" judicial scrutiny to which government sex-classification policies are subject.

2

Bathroom Bouncers

Sex-Segregated Restrooms

On June 24, 2007, Khadijah Farmer, her girlfriend, and a friend decided to stop by for a meal at the Caliente Cab, a restaurant and bar in New York City, after spending the day taking in the city's annual Lesbian, Gay, Bisexual and Transgender (LGBT) Pride celebration. Farmer, an African American out-lesbian, excused herself from the table to use the restroom. As she approached the women's restroom, a person exiting it told her that she was entering the wrong bathroom. Farmer assured the person that she was in right place.

While she was using a toilet in a locked stall, one of the restaurant's male bouncers barged into the women's restroom. He pounded his fist on the door of the stall occupied by Farmer, barking that there had been a report of a man in the women's restroom. In recounting the sequence of events, she recalls seeing him through the small space in the door frame. "That horrified me, and it made me feel extremely uncomfortable." She told him that she was female, and in the right bathroom. She opened the door, and offered to show the bouncer her female-marked New York state identification card. But the bouncer refused to look at it. "His exact words were, 'Your ID is neither here nor there.'" And then he ordered her to leave the premises immediately.[1]

The bouncer's refusal to look at Farmer's state identification card is testament to the tremendous discretionary power he had as an administrative agent. When he heard Farmer's voice, he likely "knew" that Farmer was a woman, and that the report of a "man in the ladies' bathroom" had been false. The same dissonance between appearance and voice confounded the bus driver whose disbelieving stare tracked

Christian Lovehall all the way to the back of the bus. It was a stare so intense that it had prevented him from putting the bus in gear. Lovehall's account of the incident, which I presented in the introduction, bears repeating: "So, he's looking at me, but he's hearing me 'cause out of my mouth is coming a female voice, but he sees a young boy. To him, he sees a young boy."[2]

I can personally relate to these experiences. I was often perceived as a boy and then a young man in the women's restrooms I used prior to my sex-identity transition to male. As previously discussed, sometimes— but not always—my female-sounding voice was enough to undo the misunderstanding. Not infrequently, my accuser became angrier upon hearing my voice and getting a closer look at me. In Farmer's situation, it seemed that the bouncer had already made up his mind to use his authority to override her self-statement. And now caught up in the momentum of "bouncing" her from the bar, he was also committed to not seeing, and so effectively overriding, what the state of New York had to say about her sex identity. Perhaps no one wants to be "corrected" in a public restroom.

A government-issued identity document being physically cast aside throws a sizable wrench into the logic of North Carolina's "Bathroom Bill" that was signed into law in 2016. The law, also known as HB2 (House Bill 2), mandates that people use the sex-segregated restroom that matches their "biological sex" in public schools and agencies within the state of North Carolina. The law defined "biological sex" as the sex listed on a person's birth certificate.[3] Its enforcement would require that everyone carry their birth certificate with them and be ready to show it to a bathroom bouncer stationed outside all public restrooms covered by the law. But the symbolism of HB2 is so powerful that it need not be practically enforced to get its point across.

The point was to legally ground the long-standing social custom of public restroom sex segregation in something sturdy, something original and immutable. State-issued birth certificates seemed to fit the bill. But the lawmakers failed to take into account the fact that North Carolina and every other state except for Tennessee allows transgender people to alter the sex marker on their birth certificate. So, ironically the law does not even accomplish the transgender exclusion its proponents intended. What the authors of HB2 were really saying to transgender people was, "We don't want to *see* you in public restrooms because we don't want to see you in public." Farmer effectively encountered a "bathroom bouncer" at the Caliente Cab. The bouncer's security duties included other tasks, but he was poised to step into the role of a bathroom sentinel at a moment's notice. In that role, he wasn't interested in her "biological sex" or her female-marked state identification card. Her New York state identification card was "neither here nor there."

"I'm Supposed to Be Here"

The enforcement of sex-segregated bathrooms is not really about what our birth certificates say about our sex. Instead, it's about the many normative gender stereotypes that tell us how we should appear in public as boys and girls, and men and women. The philosopher K. Anthony Appiah calls these normative stereotypes "scripts for identity."[4] North Carolina's HB2 brought the issue of "transgender discrimination" in public restrooms into the public spotlight. But sex-identity discrimination in public restrooms has been happening for a very long time. And it has mostly been happening to masculine-appearing and androgynous women, as well as to transgender women who are readable as transgender.

Farmer was twenty-eight years old when she was bounced from the Caliente Cab's female-marked bathroom. In speaking to the press about the incident, she made it clear that being reprimanded by strangers while trying to use women's public restrooms was nothing new. She told a reporter that she often got "funny looks" from other women when she was in restrooms and locker rooms with them. Those experiences were so frequent that she had a prepared statement at the ready. "I have a script that is almost routine," she said, "I say, 'I am a woman, and I'm supposed to be here.'"[5]

In their work as a writer, performer, and activist, Ivan Coyote details a lifetime of similar bathroom trouble. (Coyote's preferred gender pronoun is "they," eschewing the binary options of "he" or "she.") As a white gender-nonconforming person, Coyote relates numerous accounts of being gender policed. As with Farmer, Coyote's traumatic experiences of being questioned in women's restrooms were frequent and expected:

> I try to remind myself of that every time a nice lady in her new pantsuit for travelling screams or stares at me, I try to remember that this is maybe her first encounter with someone who doesn't appear to be much of a lady in the ladies' room. That she has no way of knowing this is already the sixth time this week that this has happened to me, and that I have four decades of it already weighing heavy on my back. She doesn't know I have been verbally harassed in women's washrooms for years. She doesn't know I have been hauled out with my pants still undone by security guards and smashed over the head with a giant handbag once. She can't know that I have five cities and seven more airport bathrooms and eleven shows left to get through before I can safely pee in my own toilet.[6]

Coyote is being too magnanimous. Most women know full well that masculine-appearing, -sounding, and -acting women exist, so it is disingenuous, at best, to be surprised to see such women in a women's restroom. To invoke the gender theorist Jack Halberstam again, our concepts of "man" and "woman" are in fact extremely elastic. Even as many people's appearances deviate from feminine and masculine ideals, sometimes considerably, we still recognize them as female and male. And at this point in our culture, most people know that transgender women and men also exist, so it is disingenuous to feign surprise upon seeing a transgender person in public. To see transgender people in public means that we should expect to see them in public restrooms.

For children, much of their time being in public is spent attending school with other kids. When Coy Mathis, a transgender girl, was in kindergarten, her Colorado school permitted her to use the girls' bathroom. However, midway through her first-grade year, school officials changed their makeshift policy. They told Coy and her parents that she could no longer use the girls' bathroom. Instead, she would have to use the boys' bathroom or a gender-neutral bathroom that had been designated for staff use only.[7] Coy's parents filed a legal complaint with the Colorado Division of Civil Rights claiming that the school district had discriminated against Coy based on her "gender expression." She won her case. Colorado Director Steven Chavez wrote, "Telling [Coy] that she must disregard her identity while performing one of the most essential human functions . . . creates an environment that is objectively and subjectively hostile."[8]

Nicole Maines, a transgender girl in Maine, sued her elementary school for its ad hoc approach to securing her right to use the restroom that felt most right to her. Maines had been allowed to use the girls' bathroom in her elementary school until a cisgender male student entered the girls' bathroom in protest of the school's policy. The school district switched course under the pressure of the controversy this stirred. Their solution was to tell Maines to begin using a gender-neutral single-stall bathroom at her middle school. The Maine Supreme Judicial Court ruled that the school had discriminated against Maines in violation of the state's ban on sexual orientation discrimination, which includes "gender identity" discrimination.[9]

The consequences of this kind of sex-identity discrimination are far from trivial. To be in public, let alone participate in public institutions on equal terms, we must have access to toilets at consistent intervals several times daily. This is a basic fact of life that we are loath to talk about openly as a culture because of our repressive social ban on discussing our bodily functions in public. Being forced to hold one's urine and bowel movements until returning home to one's own toilet is both humiliating and detrimental to one's health. In a 2008 survey of self-identified transgender people living in Washington, D.C., 70 percent of respondents said they had been "denied access, verbally harassed, or physically assaulted in public restrooms."[10]

Our laws and policies mirror this social constipation by severely restricting where and when we can relieve ourselves and tend to our bodily excretions, and those of people in our care, such as children and adults who require assistance because of age or disability. Local ordinances prohibiting urination and defecation on common public property such as parks, streets, and subway stations mean that we must have access to restrooms in the places where we work, the schools we attend, and the businesses we patronize. Because urination and defecation are life-sustaining bodily functions, people without consistent access to public restrooms are prevented from being in public for extended periods of time.[11] The fact that most public restrooms are segregated according to binary sex is a further restriction on our capacity to be and participate in the public sphere, but one that many of us accept as a necessary and harmless form of sex differentiation.

Sex-Identity Discrimination

After being ejected from the Caliente Cab restaurant, Khadijah Farmer took legal action. Although she did not self-identify as transgender, the Transgender Legal Defense and Education Fund took her case and filed a lawsuit on her behalf against the restaurant. The lawsuit alleged that the restaurant had engaged in four kinds of illegal discrimination: "gender expression" and sexual orientation discrimination in violation of New York City's Human Rights Law, and sex and sexual orientation discrimination in violation of New York State's Human Rights Law.

New York City's Human Rights Ordinance defines "gender expression" as "the representation of gender as expressed through, for example, one's name, choice of pronouns, clothing, haircut, behavior, voice, or body characteristics. Gender expression may not be distinctively male or female and may not conform to traditional gender-based stereotypes assigned to specific gender identities."

The law defines "sexual orientation" to mean "heterosexuality, homosexuality or bisexuality" and "gender" to "include *actual or perceived* sex and shall also include a person's gender identity, self-image, appearance, behavior or expression, whether or not that gender identity, self-image, appearance, behavior or expression is different from that traditionally associated with the legal sex assigned to that person at birth."[12] New York State's public accommodation antidiscrimination law defines sexual orientation as "heterosexuality, homosexuality, bisexuality or asexuality, *whether actual or perceived*" (emphasis added).

The state law also bans public accommodation discrimination on the basis of gender, but does not provide a definition of the term.[13] The multiple and intersecting sex-related harms laid out in this legal narrative of injury are useful to the extent that they complicate our understanding of the sexism experienced by Farmer. But the narrative is incomplete because it fails to identify the sex-segregated restrooms at the restaurant as the ultimate cause of this sexism.

The terms "actual" and "perceived" are critical components to contemplate in the broader understanding of sex-identity discrimination. It is not clear whether the patron who reported Farmer to the restaurant management perceived her to be a transgender man, a cisgender man, or a masculine-appearing lesbian. The same goes for the bouncer. As is true in many cases of discrimination, it is difficult and sometimes impossible to discern the true intentions of the person or group of people charged with acting in discriminatory ways.

Recall the bouncer's stern words to Farmer: there had been *a report* of a man in the women's restroom. He had interpreted the report as demanding swift action. Hence, the fist pounding on the toilet stall door. He was doing his job by investigating and enforcing the restaurant's sex-segregated bathroom policy. The report had been wrong. Ironically, the bouncer himself turned out to be the only "actual" man in the women's restroom. Farmer said she was female and in the right place. But her statements, along with her sex-marked ID, were rejected. The real accusation levied against Farmer was that she had violated heteronorma-tive standards of femininity in the eyes of another customer and then a bouncer, both of whom perceived her as being too masculine to be in the women's restroom.

The category of sexual orientation raises similar interpretive issues about perception and actuality. We know that Farmer self-identified as a lesbian based upon what she told her lawyers, and the media that cov-ered the case. New York State's antidiscrimination law includes "hetero-sexuality, homosexuality, bisexuality, and asexuality, *whether actual or perceived.*" New York City's antidiscrimination law covers "heterosexu-ality, homosexuality, or bisexuality." It lacks the explicit qualification of "actual or perceived," yet this is implied. Sexual orientation refers to the sex identity of the person or people we sexually desire, but we generally don't require evidence of particular sex acts as proof of "actual" sexual orientation. Instead, we typically take a person at the person's word when it comes to being lesbian, gay, or bisexual.

The reason that the adjective "perceived" is sometimes added to these antidiscrimination laws is because sexual orientation discrimination is often based upon the perception that someone is gay or lesbian based upon gender stereotypes. Homophobia is more about policing gender norms than policing "actual" same-sex sexual activity.[14] The masculine-appearing woman is stereotyped as lesbian, regardless of her actual or self-declared sexual orientation. The feminine-appearing man is stereo-typed as gay, regardless of his actual sexual desires and/or actions.

The final legal cause of action in Farmer's lawsuit was "gender" dis-crimination. However, the law never defines "gender." This is consistent with the wording of many other laws barring sex or gender discrimina-tion. For instance, neither Title VII nor Title IX, which ban sex discrim-ination in employment and education, respectively, define "sex," thus leaving it to courts to interpret its meaning. Through analogical reason-ing, courts have defined sex as being *like* race on the presumption that it is an immutable, visible characteristic that we are born with and can-not change. Unlike other physiological immutable characteristics such as eye color, race and sex are thought to be indelible marks of historical and ongoing social disadvantage. This is why courts treat government racial policies with the highest level of scrutiny and sex policies with an intermediate level of scrutiny.

Transgender experience, in all of its variation, challenges the presumption of sex immutability. But this mutability has not been directly incorporated into the wording of most sex discrimination laws or the interpretation of these laws in court rulings and administrative guidelines. The descriptions of gender, gender expression, and sexual orientation in New York City's and New York State's human rights laws are helpful in their attempts to expand our legal understanding of sex-related harm. But it would be even more helpful if these more complicated sex-related experiences of discrimination were explicitly included under the basic category of "sex" discrimination. This would provide a clearer guide for what restaurants and other organizations should do to assess whether and how they ought to administrate sex.

If Farmer had self-identified as transgender, or the restaurant patron and/or bouncer had used the term "transgender" or an anti-transgender slur such as "he-she" in their questioning and reprimand of Farmer, then her lawyers might also have added "gender identity" discrimination to her legal narrative of harm. Both New York City's and New York State's nondiscrimination laws ban gender identity discrimination, and they both qualify this kind of discrimination as actual or perceived. We think of "transgender discrimination" as animus aimed at people who are *in fact* in the process or have changed their birth sex from male to female, or female to male. But this is not necessarily true. We might guess, but we cannot know for certain.

Being Seen

Many people are overconfident that they can "detect" transgender people in the public sphere. However, many gender-conforming "transgender" people are not perceived as being transgender in public. In my nine years of living as a transgender man, not once has anyone questioned my presence, let alone tried to bounce me from a men's restroom. Much of this is due to the choices I've made. I could afford and chose to undergo a bilateral mastectomy, and I have access to a medical practitioner who prescribes and monitors my use of testosterone. And I follow mainstream conventions for how a professional middle-age man should dress and act in public. But my ability to make these decisions is made possible by the fact that women's gender choices are policed much more harshly and consistently than are men's.

Racial perception also plays a part in how our sex identities are perceived in public. We rarely notice someone's sex without also noticing and interpreting her or his race. When Farmer was accused of being a man in a women's restroom, she was more pointedly accused of being a black man in a women's restroom. Even more pointedly, she was accused of being a young dark-skinned black man who was deemed threatening and out of place in a female-marked public space. Sex-identity discrimination is about intersectional sexual affinity, about where and with whom we belong in the racialized social scheme of sex. In her book *Visible Identities*, philosopher Linda Alcoff observes, "What I can see for myself is what is real; all else that vies for the status of the real must be inferred from that which can be seen [and] race and gender operate as our penultimate visible identities."[15]

Being seen as a brown or black man in US society differs from being seen as a white man in this society. Navigating public space as a "butch lesbian" differs from navigating public space as a black transgender man. Lovehall shares the following account:

> Shortly after the killing of Trayvon Martin, I was approached by two white male police officers after crossing a street late one night in South Philly. They stopped me for jay-walking. Moments later, they were pushing my small frame down to the concrete, handcuffing me, and throwing me into the back of their police wagon—which smelled of urine, feces, blood and vomit—where they made me wait, wait, and wait. Eventually

they gave me two tickets and one citation totaling $360 in fines; one for jay-walking, one for not having an updated address on my ID, and one for disorderly conduct. I realized that night that I was finally "passing" as a black man. I also came to realize that the duties of the police to "protect and serve" did not necessarily apply to someone like me—young, black and male.[16]

I've been spared (so far) this harrowing experience of police violence.

But I can relate to the distressing feeling of being seen as young, black, and male.

It was a Saturday and I was in my office on campus putting the finishing touches on an article I had written. I needed to use the bathroom. I could have used the men's room on my floor, but I was still reticent about the prospect of encountering a male colleague. It was early in my transition. So, I took the elevator six flights up. I used the key I had been given to access the office where the special "single-user" restroom that had been assigned to me was located. After exiting, a white woman yelled at me from down the hall, "Who are you, and why are you here?" I was startled. I had not seen this person on my way into the office. I did not recognize her as a faculty member. Maybe she was a graduate student from another department? Her voice vibrated with fear and anger. In reminded me of the way my instructor at the feminist dojo in Brooklyn had taught us to scream defiance in the face of a male attacker back in the mid-1990s. Had I become the "male attacker" in this woman's mind in 2008?

It set me back on my heels. The condescending reprimands hurled at me as a masculine-appearing kid and adult when I tried to use women's restrooms all came surging back. My mind raced to make sense of the situation. It was a Saturday in the summer. I was wearing shorts and a T-shirt. Did that make me seem out of place in this white woman's eyes? But many of my white colleagues wear similar clothing, and do not fear being reported to campus security. I was not arrested. I was not thrown into a rancid police wagon with other suspects who'd been rounded up for petty crimes. Still, like Lovehall, I felt "hurt, angry, lost and unsafe." I called my best friend, a black non-transgender professor at another college. He listened and simply said, "Welcome."

Sex-Based Disadvantage

Women who consistently perform a certain kind of femininity can escape the sex-identity discrimination described above. But they cannot escape the sex-based disadvantage that all sex-segregated bathrooms generate. Feminists have treated public restrooms as a political issue for a very long time.

The first feminist efforts related to public toilets focused on pushing for the basic provision of women's restrooms in public so that women could be in public as workers, students, and consumers.[17] The political nature of restroom provision is clear. A very effective way of excluding someone from being in the public sphere, let alone participating in it on equal terms, is to deny the person access to toilets in that sphere. "The lack of toilet provision for women, as many feminist writers have long argued, was no oversight but part of systemic restriction of women's access to the city of man."[18]

When no public restrooms are available, women are disadvantaged in relation to men because it is easier for people who pee through penises to covertly pee illegally in various secluded public spaces, such as in alleys, behind garbage dumpsters, on the side of the road, and in plastic containers while in cars. (But not all men can urinate standing up. Peeing standing up is a feature of hegemonic masculinity.) As previously noted, being forced to "hold" one's urine can cause urinary tract infections and other health problems. Thus, women who ventured into public were vulnerable to these physical harms, which effectively became a sex-specific tax or undue burden on their civil right to be in public space, at all.

The second feminist project concerning restrooms focused on the problem of *substantive* inequality between men and women's restrooms.

Substantive equality refers to equal outcomes, and is sometimes referred to by political theorists as "egalitarianism." Procedural equality, by contrast, refers to formal statements of equal opportunity. One could argue that our current system of sex-segregated restrooms satisfies the principle of formal equality, as both males and females are given a restroom.

However, this arrangement is not substantively equal because, on average, women spend more time accessing and using their assigned public restrooms than do men. This is largely because of urinals in men's restrooms, the mechanics of peeing standing up versus sitting down, and the time needed to tend to menstruation. This time-based disadvantage can be visually verified by paying attention to the long lines of women waiting to use the restrooms in a number of public venues, while men zip in and out of their restroom aided by the time-saving technology of urinals.

In addition to requiring more time, women have often been forced to spend more time than men because they have had to travel greater distances than men to use ad hoc female-designated restrooms in workplaces where there are very few women, or just one woman. Female pioneers in male-dominated professions recount having to walk to a different floor or even building to use a women's restroom. The Supreme Court Building did not have a women's restroom until 1994, when Sandra Day O'Connor joined the bench.

At first glance, the issue of time-based inequality seems to disadvantage only women. But urinals also disadvantage men who cannot or do not wish to use them. Some transgender men can urinate standing up at a urinal, and some cannot. Some cisgender men cannot pee standing up for health reasons, or because of a physical disability. Older men with enlarged prostates that make urination difficult may forego urinals for toilets to have some privacy. Men of all ages who have certain illnesses may be told by their medical providers to urinate sitting down. Approximately 40 percent of cisgender men cannot use urinals due to anxiety, or what we might colloquially refer to as being "pee shy." Many women also experience this anxiety and cannot urinate while others are present even when using a toilet stall.[19] Men with small penises may have trouble urinating standing up. And generally speaking, some men do not wish to pee standing up at urinals because they are self-conscious about the size or appearance of their penises and fear being seen and judged by other men.

Substantive inequality also occurs when female-designated restrooms are less well maintained than male-designated restrooms, and vice versa, relating to, for instance, a lack of soap, toilet paper, running water, or cleanliness. One could further argue that substantive sex-based equality requires the provision of tampons and menstrual pads, not just for female-appearing women, but also for transgender men and gender queer people who menstruate. The prohibition against entering the opposite-sex bathroom makes monitoring these matters very difficult. You must be brazen enough to enter both restrooms, and do so repeatedly, as custodial supplies and cleanliness fluctuate over time. A sex-based disadvantage approach to restroom equality is therefore not just incomplete, but also futile. The limited feminist project of trying to make sex-segregated public restrooms separate *and* equal has been, and continues to be, an illusive ideal that can never be fully and finally achieved.

There are similarities between this country's once legalized practice of separating public-sphere restrooms according to race and the persistent legalized practice of separating these facilities according to sex. But there are some important differences between these two legalized practices, as well. Like racially segregated restrooms, sex-segregated restrooms are often substantively unequal, as pointed out above. "Colored" toilets were often nothing more than filthy outhouses at substantial distance from white restrooms that were equipped with indoor plumbing. This inequity was deliberate. Without it, the whole argument that blacks were inferior to whites would fall apart.

Unlike the call to overturn racially segregated restrooms on the basis that racial separation is inherently unequal because it is demeaning, the call to equalize male and female restrooms presumes that sex segregation is necessary, and that equalization within this segregated system is possible. Legalized sex segregation is thought to be different from Jim Crow laws because such segregation is intermittent, rather than all-encompassing. Women are not barred from most public accommodations, just the male restrooms within such accommodations.

The architecture that women must navigate in the standard American public restroom and the socially constructed beauty and socializing practices that take place in female-designated bathrooms also structure and enable sex-identity policing. Women, on average, spend more time than men in front of mirrors tending to beauty rituals such as hair brushing and makeup applying, which increases the opportunity to watch other women enter and exit individual stalls. The fact that women are forced to spend far greater amounts of time than men waiting in lines to use bathroom stalls also creates an environment where women have prolonged opportunities to visually inspect and evaluate the appearances of other women attempting to access female-designated restrooms. When I was a masculine-appearing girl and then woman, these moments spent waiting in line with other women filled me with anxiety. I was often stared at for long periods of time. Sometimes, a staring face would move in my direction, and I braced for the impact of an indignant rebuke: "This is the women's line."

Sex-segregated public restrooms also pose logistical problems for caregivers who are in the public sphere with children and adults who need assistance using toilets. Mothers who are in the public sphere with their young sons must violate sex-segregated bathroom policies by taking them into either the women's restroom or the men's room. Fathers face a similar problem when they are with their young daughters in public. Teachers and daycare workers who chaperone young children on fieldtrips must also deal with this dilemma, as do the paid and unpaid caretakers of elderly and/or disabled adults. On the surface, this seems to be a problem that equally disadvantages both women and men. However, in practice, the stereotype of male sexual predation places additional burdens on male caregivers. How would members of the public react to a male teacher taking a group of kindergarten girls into a men's room at the local zoo or children's museum?

As a practical matter, sex-segregated restrooms are also an expensive and inefficient use of space. In addition to the sexist harms discussed above, there are self-interested economic reasons for organizations to transform their existing sex-segregated restrooms into all-gender restrooms, and to work with bathroom architects to imagine and build new no-gender restrooms in radically different ways that better meet our reasonable expectations for substantive equality and a modicum of privacy and relative safety, while at the same time maximizing office, retail, and educational space. I offer some ideas for better "livable design" in the final section of this chapter.

Privacy

The defenders of sex-segregated restrooms typically justify them by invoking personal privacy, safety, and putative sex differences in cleanliness. Personal privacy and safety are legitimate policy goals, but they require contextual definition and qualification; cleanliness is another story. We have a reasonable expectation of some degree of physical seclusion from others when using public toilets, showers, and changing rooms, but this privacy is not absolute and is very different from the kind of privacy we might have in our home. Sex segregation is not necessary for ensuring this temporary seclusion in either venue. Safety is a legitimate policy goal to strive for, but it is not something that can ever be guaranteed. Indeed, believing otherwise can give us a dangerous false sense of security. There are better ways of achieving the legitimate policy goals of personal privacy and of striving for safety that are more effective, and that minimize sex-identity discrimination.

Some women claim that men are, by and large, much messier than women, and that women should not have to suffer the messiness of men in accessing public-sphere bathrooms. Some men accept this claim. But anyone who has experienced both men's and women's public restrooms, as many transgender people have, can dispel that stereotype. Neither men nor women have a monopoly on cleanliness when it comes to the places where we urinate and defecate in semi-seclusion with others in public. This is especially true of the high-volume restrooms found at highway rest stops, airports, bus and train stations, and stadiums. And even if men's restrooms were less clean than women's restrooms, it is not clear why that is a good reason to accept the status quo. If men shared restrooms with women, perhaps they would be peer-pressured into keeping public restrooms cleaner. A basic level of sanitation is a very legitimate administrative aim, but not one that is rationally related to sex segregation.

We have a reasonable expectation of some degree of privacy and safety in using public restrooms, but we should be conscientious of the ways in which race, sex, and class stereotypes infuse these aspirations. When we seek privacy we have in mind particular people we do not wish to be seen by, or be in close proximity to. When we seek safety, we have in mind particular people and situations that make us feel threatened and in danger.[20] In the case of public restrooms, safety has been framed as a matter of women and children being vulnerable to male sexual predators. The race-sex profiling of black men in the public sphere does not stop at the doors of public restrooms. Black men continue to be stereotyped as sexual predators who specifically seek out white middle- and upper-class women and children as their victims. These stereotypes are deeply ingrained in this country's history.

A dominant justification for legalized racial segregation was the stereotype that any social intermingling would give black men sexual access to white women, especially upper-class white women. As the presumed sexual partners of black men, black women were stereotyped as carriers of "venereal" diseases. Many white women workers participated in labor strikes against the racial integration of their workplaces during the 1950s on the grounds that they would have to share bathrooms with black women, which they believed would make them susceptible to contracting syphilis from shared toilet seats and towels.[21] The idea that one can contract a sexually transmitted disease from a toilet seat or towel has been debunked. Nonetheless, racist-sexist stereotypes about blacks as sources of sexual predation and contamination persist. The intimate setting of public restrooms heightens such discomfort. Whose comfort is prioritized is a matter of justice.

Safety

As with "privacy" we need to get specific about what we really mean by safety in public-sphere restrooms. I agree that policy makers and administrative agents should strive to make public restrooms as safe as possible for all users. At the same time, safety is an elusive goal when it comes to being in the public sphere, as terrorist attacks and other forms of criminal assault make all too clear. I agree with the writer Roxane Gay that "safety" is better conceived in its progressive tense of "striving" than as a fait accompli.[22] We can *hope* and *work* to make particular environments, including restrooms, safer, but it is a mistake to expect to always *be* safe in these facilities. Just as we should remain vigilant as we go about our business in the public sphere, we should remain vigilant when we use public-sphere restrooms.

The mistaken belief that sex segregation ensures safety actually makes female-designated restrooms more dangerous for all women. When I presented my critique of sex-segregated restrooms to a group of college students, an audience member mentioned that she had been stalked by a male, and found that the women's restroom was one of the only places where she could escape him. I take this objection seriously, but it is flawed in at least two ways. First, sex-segregated restrooms serve this function only if one's stalker is of the opposite sex. And second, as the predator is already breaking laws in stalking the victim, he will likely break another law to enter a women's restroom with little or no hesitation.

Tragically, this is what happened in a Las Vegas casino in 1997 when a man followed a girl into a women's restroom and raped and murdered her.[23] The goal of minimizing violence is reasonable and important, but restroom sex segregation is not rationally related to achieving this goal. Even worse, the misconception of women's restrooms as places of refuge lulls many women into a false and dangerous sense of personal safety when they enter those rooms.

As political theorist and transgender activist Paisley Currah describes, "the new transgender panic" is the false stereotype that transgender women are *really* men who pretend to be women so that they can enter women's restrooms to commit sexual assault. There have not been any reported incidents whereby a transgender woman has sexually assaulted another woman in a women's bathroom. Yet the myth persists and drives policy making. Defending North Carolina's "Bathroom Bill," state senator David Brock said, "You know, $42,000 is not going to cover the medical expenses when a pervert walks into a bathroom and my little girls are there."[24]

When it comes down to it, the privacy and safety we can expect in public restrooms are heavily circumscribed by the fact that we are *in public*. We are not really privatized in our bodily functions since our own excretions are audible and can be smelled by others. Most of today's toilet stalls do not have floor-to-ceiling partitions because of cost and to make mopping floors easier, and the gaps between the door and frame allow us to see in and out of stalls, which further diminishes visual seclusion. Farmer could see the male bouncer as he pounded on the door of the stall she occupied, and he could see her. If we understand the idea of privacy as being prevented from seeing or smelling other people's filth, our current sex-segregated restrooms do a poor job of ensuring bodily privacy for everyone. This aversion to the public airing of bodily waste and odor also drives bathroom policy.

And while it may be legitimate for a business to limit the use of its restrooms to customers, such policies are often used to single out people who appear to be homeless or teenagers unaccompanied by adults, on the assumption that they cannot be customers, or that they are not the *kind* of customers that the business wants to attract. Have you ever used a Starbucks restroom under the pretense of being a customer?

Why Correction Won't Solve the Problem

The mainstream transgender civil rights strategy has been to assimilate and accommodate transgender and gender-nonconforming individuals into existing sex-segregated public restrooms without questioning the harmfulness of sex segregation itself. The Caliente Cab restaurant adopted this definition of equality in its out-of-court settlement with Farmer. As part of its settlement, the restaurant chain agreed to add gender identity and expression to its corporate nondiscrimination policy, institute a gender-neutral dress code for its employees, and change its employee handbook to state that all patrons and employees of the restaurant have the right to use "the bathroom facilities consistent with their gender identity and expression."[25] Bouncers, managers, wait staff, and patrons are no longer authorized to say who may and may not use the sex-segregated restrooms in the restaurant.

The managerial decision not to enforce sex segregation seems like a step in the right direction. But there are some problems with this approach. The policy does not prevent customers from questioning and harassing other customers within and outside of the sex-segregated restrooms. The "men" and "women" signs on restroom doors effectively deputize anyone to make a citizen's arrest. The fact that the citizen's arrest would not trigger official ejection from the restroom once the alleged violation was reported to a restaurant employee is cold comfort to the person who has already been humiliated by the accusation. Moreover, the patchwork of different policies across the city, state, and country means that people such as Farmer never know when or where they might be harassed and/or ejected from the restrooms they need in order to be in public.

The assimilationist approach was used to settle a 2011 case in which a ninth-grade white female-to-male transgender student brought a Title IX sex-discrimination federal lawsuit against the Arcadia Unified School District in California. The student alleged that school district officials had engaged in illegal sex discrimination when they denied his request to use the male restroom and locker facilities at his school. As with the Caliente Cab lawsuit, the case was settled out of court in the student's favor. As part of the legal settlement, the Departments of Justice and Education both wrote letters stating that discrimination on the basis of "gender identity" constitutes sex discrimination in violation of Title IX. Officials from both departments were quick to caution that the content of the letters should not be construed as either agency's official policy.[26]

The settlement gave this particular student what he and his parents wanted: permission to use the boys' restroom at his school. But this kind of remedy will benefit only transgender students who can and will conform to one binary sex category. A significant factor in the Arcadia case was the fact that the transgender male student visually and socially fit into his male peer group. He had identified as male for several years, had adopted a traditionally male name, and had the support of his parents and teachers.

But relying on social acceptance sets a precarious precedent for extending civil rights to transgender people. How will the school district handle a case in which a student self-identifies as neither male nor female, or as both male and female? Or, to follow the logic of the case, would the case have been so compelling, and clearly seen as sex discrimination, if the transgender student had not been accepted as male by his parents, teachers, and classmates? Would school officials have reacted differently if the transgender student had been black, working class, and/or poor? As we've seen, the people who are the most vulnerable to sex-identity policing and persecution are those whose sex identities are not socially affirmed in the schools they attend, the places they work, and the businesses they patronize.

Wherever a sex-classification policy remains in place, administrative decisions must be made about its enforcement, and such administration introduces the potential for sex-identity discrimination. In school districts, teachers and administrators will have to make decisions about which students' transgender identities are "sincere." And it is likely that they will use the ability and/or desire of the student to conform to race-

and class-specific male or female standards as the de facto criteria for making those decisions. Transgender experience tells us that the categories of male and female are mutable, and intersex experience tells us that the dyadic sex categories of male or female are insufficient. Hence, the sex-identity decisions and appearances of others do not always conform to our expectations.

The lack of stable criteria for enforcing sex segregation has not deterred politicians from claiming that they have found such criteria. Utah became the first state to have a bill introduced in its state assembly calling for the enforcement of sex-segregated restrooms in public schools. In 2014, a Republican state representative introduced a bill that would legally require public school students to use the sex-segregated restroom that corresponds to their "gender." The bill defined gender as "the male or female phenotype" of a person that is recorded on a birth certificate or stated in a letter from a physician "based on a physical inspection of the person's genitalia." The bill did not deny the existence of "transgender" students, but relegated them to use "reasonable alternate-bathroom accommodations" if so requested by such a student. The bill defined "transgender" students as people whose "gender identity" does not match their "gender."[27] The bill ignited national media attention, but was never passed into law. A Florida state representative introduced a similar bill in 2015. As of this writing, North Carolina is the only state to have enacted such legislation.[28]

North Carolina's "Bathroom Bill" is irrational, draconian, and patently discriminatory. But the demarcation of separate restrooms for males and females follows the same misguided logic: that sex is binary, original, and natural, stable over time, and visually obvious based upon whether you appear right now to have appeared at birth to have a penis or a vagina. In an eerie illustration of gender theorist Judith Butler's famous statement that "gender is a kind of imitation for which there is no original,"[29] we see conservative politicians rifling through government-issued bureaucratic paperwork to find something that can never be found: the final truth about where we belong in the social scheme of binary sex. For that information we must defer to the present-day self-statements of those with whom we share public space, including public restrooms. Khadijah Farmer, Ivan Coyote, Coy Mathis, and Nicole Maines should have been taken at their word.

Another approach to addressing the problem of transgender discrimination caused by sex-segregated restrooms has been accommodation. This has meant adding another purpose to existing single-user bathrooms that were built to meet Americans with Disabilities Act (ADA) requirements, or including such third restrooms in newly constructed public-sphere buildings. Some of these third bathrooms have also been designated as "family restrooms" that allow parents to accompany and assist their children. In the case of new construction, accommodation can take the form of mandating that newly constructed public-sphere buildings include a third gender-neutral, single-user bathroom. In 2011, the city of Philadelphia, which has been commended for its LGBT-inclusive laws and policies, passed a bill that requires all newly constructed city-owned buildings to include single-user gender-neutral bathrooms in addition to traditional sex-segregated restrooms. The announcement of this "trans-inclusive" legislation received high praise from mainstream and progressive media.[30] Evanston, Illinois, recently adopted an ordinance that requires all single-user public accommodation restrooms to be designated "all gender," with appropriate signage to so indicate.[31]

This approach is based upon a disability rights model of "reasonable accommodation." The ADA requires restrooms in workplaces, public areas, and schools to be accessible to "individuals with disabilities," where disability is defined as "a physical or mental impairment that substantially limits one or more major life activities." When it is "technically infeasible" for an accommodation to be made, the ADA allows that "unisex (or single-user) toilet rooms" are sufficient. The ADA does not require disabled people to use the single-user restroom, or a modified stall within a sex-segregated restroom.[32] Similarly, Philadelphia's ordinance does not require transgender individuals to use the single-user restroom.

The problem with this approach is that it fails to recognize sex segregation as the primary source of sex-identity discrimination. Even worse, the creation of a third restroom option that is set physically apart from the men's and women's restrooms fortifies the principle of sex segregation as normal. The designation of a separate restroom stigmatizes transgender identities by telling transgender people that we are exceptional. And in doing so, it sanctions and reinforces the prejudice of many people who view transgender people as too "aesthetically shocking" to share a public restroom with.[33]

As disability rights activists make plain, "accommodation" is a relative term that enables those of us in the "normal" category to forget the many ways in which policies and the built environment are made to *accommodate us*.[34] Liberal accommodation is conducive to conservative ends. The Republican Utah bill seeking to administratively enforce restroom sex segregation in public schools contained a "special accommodation" for transgender students to be permitted to use a physically separate gender-neutral bathroom. And North Carolina governor Pat McCrory said in a television interview, "We didn't pass any laws eliminating unisex bathrooms in our schools or in our private sector."[35]

Potty Parity

The corrective paradigm of accommodation has also been used both in the fight for the provision of public toilets for women and to settle lawsuits based in the substantive inequality of such facilities. Feminists were of course right to fight for public toilets. But they were wrong to accept the sexist premise that the fact that only men had been using public-sphere restrooms meant that such restrooms were in fact men's restrooms. And they were wrong to accept the proposition that the restrooms should remain so, even as women were formally integrated into public-sphere activities such as formal employment, education, and the use of public accommodations.

It might be too much to have expected first-wave feminists to buck the Victorian morality that was leading to sex segregation in so many public venues. But it is worth noting that things had once been different. Before state laws gave women a "restroom of their own," first in factories and then throughout the public sphere, working-class women had been sharing toilets with men in factories.[36] Like many forms of liberalism, this version of liberal feminism failed to question the terms of inclusion. There was nothing innately masculine or male-specific about these restrooms except for the presence of male urinals. But those and other fixtures could have been easily altered through physical renovation. We could have built the standard American public restroom very differently, but we chose not to. And we continue to choose not to do so today.

In the 1990s feminists pushed for so-called "potty parity" laws that aimed to make separate sex-segregated restrooms substantively equal on the dimension of time. These legal arguments pushed beyond a strictly formal or de jure understanding of equal opportunity, asserting that it is not enough to merely provide women a place to urinate and defecate in the public sphere; some attention must also be paid to sex-specific characteristics that result in gross time disparities in using these facilities. Time disparity was the basis of several "potty parity" court cases during the 1990s. Proposed legislative solutions to this disparity included equalizing the number of toilet stalls in women's restrooms as measured against *both* the number of toilet stalls and urinals in men's restrooms, or some other "egalitarian" ratio. In some states and municipalities, "potty parity" measures resulted in the provision of more restrooms for women in particular public-sphere venues.[37]

But these additional restrooms have not eliminated sex-based time disparity in using public restrooms. And while these efforts may have increased public awareness concerning this form of sexism, they have not changed how the vast majority of public restrooms are designed and built. And even when time disparity is taken into account, the metrics fluctuate according to the sex-identity breakdown of how particular venues are used. For example, sex-specific bathroom needs vary in a stadium depending on the event. A monster truck show is likely to skew restroom demand heavily toward men, while a figure skating competition or Justin Bieber concert is likely to skew restroom demand heavily toward women and girls, respectively. How many extra stalls are needed in women's restrooms to achieve parity in these scenarios?

As with many other aspects of gender parity, the real problem is that the original male standard has not been challenged in a serious and concerted way. In restrooms, this would mean challenging the male urinal and using the toilet stall as the standard place for everyone. But even if we could ask or force men to make this sacrifice, there would be sex-based disparity if men continued to pee standing up, and women continued to pee sitting down. While it may be practically impossible to enforce a "sit-down-only" policy, some feminists in Germany have tried to encourage this behavioral change by posting signs in bathrooms proclaiming, "Here one pees sitting down," and explaining the communal benefits of better sanitation. The signs elicited a strong response from many German men who began publicly insisting upon peeing standing up as a vital part of their masculine identity. The title of a scholarly book on the subject says it all: "Peeing Standing Up: The Last Bastion of Masculinity."[38]

Policy Redesign

A powerful solution to the range of sexism discussed in this chapter is to imagine and build restrooms very differently than we do today. Current sex-segregated restrooms could be converted into unisex or no-gender bathrooms without too much expense. An important aspect of such renovation is to consider removing urinals and building additional private stalls in their place.

Another renovation to consider would be to extend the walls of individual stalls all the way, or closer, to the floor to increase users' privacy. If a large organization with multiple restrooms is looking for a less radical reform, they might consider converting some or most of their restrooms to no-gender, while maintaining a traditional sex-segregated restroom option for those who wish to use it. When I visited Reed College in Portland, Oregon, in 2013 to give a talk, they had such a model in place in their student center building. I asked some of the students how they felt about it, and they responded with shrugs as if it were no big deal.

When it comes to new construction, an even better no-gender restroom model is to design and build a single bathroom area for all to use. Some restaurants in cities such as Philadelphia and New York have built bathrooms with all-gender single-user stalls that are enclosed by floor-to-ceiling partitions. These private stalls are built around a common area where sinks and mirrors are available for everyone, regardless of sex identity or gender expression. Transgender and cisgender parents, teachers, babysitters, and other caretakers would not have to worry about entering the "wrong" bathroom to visually keep track of or physically assist those under their care. I describe this as an even better option because it optimizes space, which is often an important factor in purchasing or leasing commercial real estate. When restaurant owners were interviewed about their decision to create one restroom space, they cited spatial concerns. The twin harms of sex-based disadvantage and sex-identity discrimination were not the driving forces in their innovation, but rather a beneficial by-product of a smart business decision.[39]

Inadvertently, this innovation in public restrooms exemplifies the concept of "universal design." This movement gained momentum in the 1970s and was inspired by the question of how to design the built environment with the needs of people with physical disabilities in mind.[40] The classic example of this design principle is curb cuts on sidewalks. This design feature emanated from the need to make sidewalks usable for people in wheelchairs. However, the benefits of curb cuts are much more far-reaching. Among those who benefit from this modification of our shared cityscape are people pushing baby strollers, people using crutches and canes, people pulling wheeled luggage, delivery people using wheeled trolleys, and people like me with short legs. The advantages are multiple and expansive, and the costs are small. There is no disadvantage to those who are not in any of the situations listed above.

What if we consciously and deliberately applied the concept of universal design to public restrooms? How might we rethink and redesign this "democratic architecture" to meet the reasonable goals of a modicum of personal privacy and safety, while simultaneously minimizing sexist harm? Universal design begins by taking into account the needs of the people who are most hindered and excluded by traditional design. In the case of restrooms this group includes people who are transgender-appearing and gender-nonconforming.

The absence of binary sex signs on restroom doors removes the mechanism that made it possible for another customer to report Farmer as "a man in the women's restroom," and for the bouncer to take the report as grounds for ejection, even in the face of a state identification card that showed her photo next to a female sex marker. At the same time, cisgender and transgender people who are gender-conforming benefit from the redesign. Many of us are in the public sphere with opposite-sex children and other adults in need of our assistance when it comes to using a public bathroom. All of us are vulnerable to needing this care work at some point in our lives.[41] So, ultimately it is in all of our interests to eliminate this long-standing obstacle to accessing and navigating the public sphere on equal terms. No one is made worse off by the redesign; the benefits are universal.

The current ADA administrative guidelines hint in the direction of universal design, noting that "unisex toilet rooms benefit people who use opposite sex personal care workers. For this reason, it is advantageous to install unisex toilet rooms in addition to accessible single-sex toilet rooms in new facilities."[42] This "advisory" guideline is more profound than it may at first appear because "opposite sex" care is not limited to persons with disabilities. The problem with this alert is that it does not mandate unisex bathrooms as a solution for making public restrooms more accessible to all of us, including people with disabilities.

Conclusion

Farmer's lawyers framed her injury of sex discrimination too narrowly. They missed an opportunity to use sex-discrimination law to locate and excavate a deeper source of sex-identity discrimination and sex-based disadvantage: sex segregation itself.

I believe we would all be better off by harnessing sex-discrimination laws to a much more expansive feminist project. That project ought to promote gender parity between men and women, as well as the individual freedom to personally change the predicates of gender parity: the categories of male and female. This civil right is especially important to those of us whose sex-identity decisions may not be socially recognized by others in places such as the restrooms we must use in the schools we attend, the places we work, and the businesses we frequent. The end of sex-segregated restrooms would not be the "end of the world," but the beginning of a brand-new world of better bathroom design.

3

Checking a Sex Box to Get into College

Single-Sex Admissions

In 2013, Calliope Wong, an Asian American transgender woman, applied for admission to Smith College, a prestigious single-sex private women's college in Massachusetts, and was rejected. It was the second time Wong had been rejected by Smith. But unlike the rejection letters received by most applicants to the prestigious women's college, Wong's letter said that she was ineligible for admission because some of the sex markers on her application materials were male. Stacy Schmiedel, Smith spokesperson, told the press, "We do require that a prospective student's application and supporting materials consistently identify her as a woman."

The first time she applied, Wong explained that the administrative staff at her high school had failed to change the sex markers on her high school transcripts and other supporting documents in time for Smith's deadline. Smith officials told Wong that she would be eligible for admission in the future as long as those "clerical errors" were corrected. Wong managed to get all of the sex markers on her academic documents changed to female. But it wasn't easy. As she explained in an interview with the cable news network MSNBC, "It was quite time-consuming [and] it took a lot of explaining for my [high school] guidance counselors and my administrative staff to correct all of my documents."[1] Nonetheless, a second rejection letter arrived from Smith. Like the first one, it said that the college would not consider her application. This time the problem was that her Free Application for Federal Student Aid (FAFSA) form still listed her sex as male.[2]

When Wong received the second rejection letter from Smith, she did what many young people in her generation would do. She shared her story on social media. Eventually, mainstream major media outlets such as the *New York Times*, *USA Today*, and *MSNBC* took notice, and the issue was debated in the national press for a short time in 2015. The incident brought to public light the fact that many private women's colleges were treating applications from transgender women on an ad hoc basis without any set policies. There were protests on Smith's campus pressuring the administration to make its admissions policies more welcoming to transgender women. Students hoisted signs that read, "Trans women belong here," "Welcome Trustees! Let's Welcome Trans ladies," and "Smith College can't be a women's college without supporting trans women."

Under pressure, the administration relented somewhat and removed the requirement that nonacademic documents such as the FAFSA be consistently marked female. But it kept the requirement that standard application documents such as high school transcripts bear female markers. Under the revised policy, Wong became eligible for admission to Smith. But it was too late. She had already accepted an admissions offer from the University of Connecticut, where she is an honors student, and declined Smith's retroactive offer of admission.[3] Did Smith do the right thing by stretching its definition of women to include Wong, or should it have abandoned its women-only admissions policy altogether?

As Wong's story of rejection became national news, other high-profile women's colleges such as Barnard, Mount Holyoke, and Mills came under similar scrutiny. Lynn Pasquerella, president of Mount Holyoke College, publicly defended the school's exclusion of men on nominal grounds. "At a women's college we have to have some criterion for admission. In addition to academic excellence, it's *being a woman*."[4] Pasquerella meant her statement to be definitive, but instead she ended up stirring the very question that resists definition: what does it mean to *be* a woman? One way to answer this question is to say that being a woman means not being a man. But of course that answer begs the question of what it means to be a man.

These questions are relevant to women's colleges, and indeed to all colleges. I would like to see single-sex colleges open their admissions processes to everyone. But in doing so, I don't believe they should abandon their important historical and continuing mission of tackling institutional sexism in US higher education. Although women now outnumber men on many college campuses, female students still suffer disadvantageous outcomes in their college experiences ranging from how often they speak out in classroom discussions to the kinds of praise and criticism they receive in letters of recommendation written by their professors and the professional networks they have access to upon graduation.

Addressing these and other forms of institutional sexism in colleges is a legitimate and important educational goal. But the exclusion of all men from admissions is not necessary for or, in the idiom of antidiscrimination law, "rationally related" to such a goal. Ironic as it may seem, requiring that prospective students check a male or female box on an application form is a poor proxy for furthering feminist institutional reform. Perhaps the time has come to rename women's colleges "historically women's colleges," in the same way that we refer to "black" colleges and universities as historically black colleges and universities (HBCUs).

Broader Implications

Single-sex college admissions may seem less consequential than the other policy venues discussed in this book. After all, single-sex colleges are few in number, and therefore directly affect a very small number of people. But the definitional question of who qualifies as a woman in a competitive college admissions process is the thin edge of a wedge onto questions that affect *all* prospective college students and their families, as well as those who work in colleges as faculty and staff. Do these institutions, both single-sex and coed, have a legitimate interest in knowing the sex identity of their applicants? If so, then should this information be required or volunteered by applicants? What definition of sex and/ or gender is being invoked when a college prompts a student to check a male or female box on an application form? How should individual colleges use this information? What is the relationship between the gathering of sex-identity information and the legitimate educational goals of specific colleges?

The overwhelming majority of today's single-sex colleges are "women's colleges," meaning that only "women" qualify for consideration in their admissions processes. As of this writing, there are forty-three private single-sex women's colleges. And just three private single-sex men's colleges remain today: Wabash, Hampden-Sydney, and Morehouse.

Some of the oldest and most prestigious women's colleges were the elite Seven Sisters colleges of the Northeast, which were chartered in the late nineteenth century before women won the right to vote. Radcliffe, Vassar, Wellesley, Smith, Mount Holyoke, Barnard, and Bryn Mawr were separate legal entities with their own charters, but each was affiliated with one or more men's Ivy League colleges. Harvard, Yale, Columbia, Brown, Princeton, Dartmouth, Cornell, and Penn began admitting women in the 1960s and 1970s under pressure from the women's liberation movement. Vassar became coed in 1969, and is the only Seven Sisters college to have done so. Radcliffe College began offering joint diplomas to female students who matriculated at Harvard beginning in 1963, and then executed a "non-merger merger" with Harvard in 1977. When I graduated from Harvard College in 1993 my diploma listed both Harvard and Radcliffe Colleges. This ended in 1999. Currently, Radcliffe exists as a non-degree-granting institute for advanced women's studies. The five other Seven Sisters colleges continue their single-sex admissions policies, and have remained private women's colleges.

Sex-Based Experience

Five years before Wong was rejected by Smith on the basis of her inconsistently sex-marked government paperwork, the *New York Times*

Magazine ran a story that profiled two white transgender men who had been admitted as women to the women-only colleges of Barnard and Wellesley, respectively. After being admitted, both students changed their sex identities to male. The story was featured on the cover of the magazine with the titillating title, "When Girls Will Be Boys." The article quoted alumnae who objected to allowing transgender male students to stay enrolled on the grounds that it was tantamount to "passively going coed."[5] Seven years later the *New York Times* ran another article on transgender men at women's colleges titled "When Women Become Men at Wellesley."[6]

The different verb tenses in these two national headlines inadvertently highlight a key issue relevant to college admissions: the timing of a person's sex-identity change or transition. Does being counted as a woman at the time of college admission necessitate past experience of *having been* a girl or having been identified by others as female? Some feminists argue that the definition of what it means to be a woman all comes down to the experience of being seen and treated as female in a patriarchal society.[7] Gender socialization runs so deep that sex-identity change later in life cannot undo it. According to this line of argument, a person who transitions from male to female has already been socialized as male, and reaped the benefits of patriarchy, and so is ineligible to claim the identity of being a woman. And a person who transitions from female to male can be doing so only in a desperate attempt to join and thereby benefit from the patriarchy.[8]

Some of the social media responses to Wong's story of being rejected by Smith made such claims. For instance, one person found and posted two photos of Wong that she described as "obviously male." She wrote,

When you read a sympathetic news article about a "young woman denied entry to a women's college," you tend to picture a young woman in your mind. As in female (at least I do). But Calliope is clearly, unambiguously male. It's hard to believe that based on her appearance, anyone would classify her as a young woman. If Calliope looked female, her presence would certainly be less disruptive. On the other hand, the point of female-only schools is to counter the effects of socialization under patriarchy. Female socialization is something Calliope, who is obviously male, could not possibly have experienced.[9]

But if female socialization is the litmus test for being considered female, then how much time lived "as female" is enough to earn one's "woman card"?

Drugs that delay the onset of puberty are now available and are being administered to some transgender children to delay the onset of secondary sex characteristics until the young person turns eighteen and can make decisions regarding surgeries and hormone therapy.[10] Recall the earlier discussed transgender children who legally battled to use the bathroom at their schools that matched their self-defined sex identity. When Coy Mathis, the five-year-old transgender girl living in Colorado, reaches the age of puberty, will she be given puberty-blocking drugs?[11] If so, then when she is old enough to apply to college, she may have spent nearly her entire life being female. Nicole Maines, the Maine teenager, might have had a less female-embodied experience than Mathis, but that depends on when she began her transition from male to female.[12] Whether a child has access to such medical treatment depends on whether that child has emotionally supportive parents or guardians who can afford such treatment. It also largely depends upon how closely each girl is able to meet hegemonic femininity standards of appearance, comportment, and speech. How much turns on physical appearance? Must a person "pass" as female in order to experience "female socialization under patriarchy"?

The thirteen-year-old transgender boy at the center of the Arcadia, California, school district lawsuit will have spent his teenage years as male, but depending on the timing of his transition, he may also have spent a significant period of his childhood as female-embodied.[13] Should he be eligible for admission to Smith or Mount Holyoke based on having lived part of his life as a female? Does it make sense to say that a transgender boy who transitions to male at the age of four or five has experienced antifemale sexism? What about people who feel and experience themselves as transgender but do not use surgeries or hormone therapy as part of their sex-identity transitions?[14] And what about prospective college students who do not self-identify as male or female, or identify as both?

Can the women-only admissions policies of women's colleges be defended on the grounds that they are a necessary form of feminist separation? From 1975 to 2016, the annual Michigan Womyn's Music Festival exemplified such a temporary respite for women. The space was dedicated to lesbian feminist cultural values. And from its inception, the festival was challenged by the question of whether transgender women should be permitted to join its community. Their "womyn-born-womyn" policy was interpreted by many to exclude transgender women on the basis that transgender women are by definition women who were designated as male at birth. Festival organizers said that the policy was merely "intentional," and that it was up to individuals to interpret the meaning of that intention for themselves. Despite this adjusted language, a transgender woman was ejected from the festival in 1991, which led several performers and supporters to withdraw from subsequent festivals. The internal debate led to some awkward and confusing statements about who counts as womyn, such as, "Trans womyn who identify as womyn-born-womyn are welcome at Michfest."[15]

Are women's colleges analogous to Michfest? Or, do these colleges discriminate against men? The way I see it, the harm generated by today's women-only colleges is more about policing the definitional borders of femaleness and maleness than it is about group-based male disadvantage in relationship to female advantage, and vice versa. Women's colleges were founded because men's colleges were unwilling to accept them. As I've suggested in previous chapters, sex-identity discrimination is about gender policing that uses raced notions of hegemonic femininity and masculinity to stipulate who belongs and does not belong in the binary categories of women and men.

Sex-identity discrimination is pervasive in everyday life, but it becomes especially intense when something socially valuable such as an elite college education or an Olympic medal (the subject of chapter 4) is at stake. Therefore it's not surprising that the mainstream media have focused on a handful of prestigious private women's colleges, rather than the majority of private women's colleges and the three remaining private men's colleges. Should these colleges be permitted to continue their tradition of single-sex education in a time when there are a variety of colleges to which individual women and men can apply?

Legal Loopholes

There is also an important legal question to consider. Why in 2016 are some colleges legally permitted to formally exclude prospective students from admission on the basis of sex, while others are not? Why did the negative publicity surrounding Wong's rejection from Smith not put an end to Smith's women-only admissions process? The legal answer lies in a special exemption that was written into Title IX. This federal law is best known for its impact on collegiate sports, but it covers all aspects and levels of federally funded educational programming, and includes students, faculty, and staff involved in such programming. Title IX states "that no person in the United States shall, *on the basis of sex*, be excluded from participation in, be denied the benefits of, or be subjected to discrimination under any educational program or activity receiving Federal financial assistance" (emphasis added).[16]

At the heart of Title IX is a presumptive ban on single-sex educational institutions because historically most of these institutions excluded girls and women based on both the false stereotype that they were not as smart as men, and the normative stereotype that they should remain in the private sphere of the home. However, the legislation exempts certain kinds of single-sex colleges from this presumptive ban. As Title IX was being debated in Congress in 1972, several elite private women's colleges such as Smith, along with colleges such as Harvard and Dartmouth, which were male-only at the time, lobbied for and won a special exemption.

The exemption allows private colleges that were founded prior to 1972 and that have "traditionally and continuously" had "a policy of admitting only students of one sex" to maintain their single-sex admissions policies.[17] This exemption applies only to undergraduate college programs, so all graduate educational programs at these institutions must be coed. Many private single-sex colleges covered by the exemption voluntarily abandoned their exclusionary admissions policies in the 1960s and 1970s. Religious colleges are exempt from Title IX and may discriminate on the basis of sex.[18] This means that religious colleges can also discriminate on the basis of transgender identity.[19]

Why is *any* college legally permitted under Title IX to use sex classification in its admissions policies at all? Why must applicants check a male or female sex-identity box on the admissions forms used by all colleges? The quick answer is that no one has questioned the legality of such bureaucratic sorting because, like the other sex-classification policies discussed in this book, it is presumed to be necessary and harmless. One could argue that the Title IX exemption should be overturned on the basis that women-only admissions disadvantage men, and men-only admissions disadvantage women. This would be analogous to cases alleging that the use of race-based affirmative action by colleges disadvantages white and Asian American students.[20]

The Supreme Court has ruled that race can be used as one of several factors in college admissions, so long as it is not used as the determining factor in such decision making. The Court has stated that race can be treated as a factor in diversity, and that diversity is a legitimate policy goal for colleges to pursue.[21] There have not, however, been any legal challenges to sex-based affirmative action in higher education. Another exemption was written into Title IX that explicitly permits private colleges, even those receiving federal funds, to use sex-based affirmative action in their admissions processes. This exemption has recently come to light as some private colleges have publicly admitted to engaging in affirmative action in favor of men because women now constitute the majority of students on many campuses.[22]

The Supreme Court has ruled on the question of whether a public college's use of a single-sex admission policy violates the Equal Protection Clause of the Fourteenth Amendment. In the 1996 landmark case *United States v. Virginia*, the Virginia Military Institute (VMI), founded in 1839, claimed that its men-only admissions policy was necessary because of tradition and constitutional because it did not disadvantage women in relationship to men. The college argued that its unique "adversative method" of training citizen soldiers would be compromised by the presence of female students. VMI created Mary Baldwin College as a separate women-only college, which it then proclaimed a "separate but equal" institution.

Justice Ginsburg, writing for the Court, countered that VMI's male-only admissions policy was unconstitutional because it used sex-role stereotypes to place "artificial constraints" on the individual opportunities of women. The Court acknowledged the statistical fact that most women are physically weaker than most men. But it argued that that statistical fact could not be used to justify the school's male-only admissions policy. Some women do seek out such an experience, and can meet its rigors. The Court rejected VMI's argument that female cadets could achieve a "separate but equal" military training at Mary Baldwin College.[23] But the Court never defined "sex" or "gender."

Is the exclusion of men from women's colleges such as Smith, Mount Holyoke, and Spelman similarly sexist? The defenders of women's colleges make a compelling argument that they are not. The harm done to women by VMI's male-only policy was material: it prevented women from accessing the social, economic, and political capital that has long been available to the men who graduate from patriarchal institutions such as VMI. Indeed, one of the facts that the Court emphasized in *United States v. Virginia* was the high number of VMI alumni who held powerful positions in Virginia's business and political leadership. VMI's goal of producing "citizen soldiers" was a euphemism for reproducing male economic and political power within the state. VMI countered this charge by invoking the libertarian claim that women had other comparable options to choose from in Virginia's higher education marketplace. The Court rightly found that argument to be disingenuous. "A purpose genuinely to advance an array of educational options is not served by VMI's historic and constant plan to afford a *unique educational benefit* only to males. However well this plan serves Virginia's sons, it makes no provision whatever for her daughters."[24]

Wong's rejection from Smith raises the question of single-sex admissions in a very different context from that of an all-male military college. It is true that many powerful women have graduated from elite women's colleges, among them Hillary Clinton, Gloria Steinem, and Madeleine Albright. Women's college alums make up 20 percent of the women in Congress and 30 percent of *Businessweek*'s list of "rising" women in corporate America, even though only 2 percent of US female college graduates attended women's colleges.[25] These impressive statistics notwithstanding, the idea that men are denied access to social, economic, and political capital in consequence of being shut out of elite women's colleges is a hard sell. Sex discrimination law protects both women and men from being disadvantaged "because of sex," but the reality is that women, as a group, have suffered disproportionately more than men when it comes to institutional and organizational sexism.

On a Mission

How do the remaining single-sex colleges defend their exclusionary admissions policies?

The mission statements of most elite single-sex women's colleges draw a causal connection between their women-only institutional identities and their educational values, goals, and benefits. For instance, Mount Holyoke's website states that it has remained a women-only college "by choice" because "we know that women thrive in an environment where all of the resources are designed for them." To substantiate this claim, the website has a link to social scientific research showing that female students earning degrees at women's colleges perform better than women graduating from coeducational colleges. They are twice as likely to earn advanced degrees, and are more likely to assume leadership roles, to speak in classroom discussion, and to report greater self-confidence.[26]

In the values statement found on its website, Smith states that it "prepares women to fulfill their responsibilities to the local, national, and global communities in which they live." Their website includes a host of answers to the question "Why is Smith a Women's College?," including, in bold font, "At Smith, women are the focus of *all* the attention and *all* the opportunities"; "At Smith, all of the leaders are women"; "At Smith, the 'old boys network' becomes an ageless women's network."[27]

On its website, Barnard describes itself as "a liberal arts college in New York City dedicated to the success of women." It highlights "the inspiring environment of a women's college," in which students get to "debate ideas with the smartest women you will ever know" in small classes.[28] Here, the link between the sex-identity makeup of the college and success is implied rather than explicit, as it is on Mount Holyoke and Smith's websites.

Of the four historically black colleges for women, only Spelman and Bennett have remained single-sex.[29] Spelman's mission statement describes the college as "a historically black college and global leader in the education of women of African descent, [that] is dedicated to academic excellence in the liberal arts and science and in the intellectual, creative, and ethical and leadership development of its students." It also mentions the strong network that its graduates have access to.[30]

In its mission statement, Bennett College describes itself as "a small, private, historically black college for women." It explicitly welcomes "students, staff, and faculty from diverse backgrounds." Prospective students are told that they will leave Bennett with "a greater appreciation of the history and culture of Africa and the African Diaspora, the struggles and accomplishments of women, and a realization of their own ability and the possibilities to help change the world."[31] While both Spelman and Bennett are legally permitted under Title IX's special provision to remain single-sex, neither college is permitted to limit its admission process on the basis of race. Instead, it emphasizes its history as a black college for women, and its present-day specialization in the "history of and culture of Africa and the African Diaspora."

The mission statements of the few remaining men's colleges are conspicuously silent on the relevance of a male-only environment to the educational outcomes they market to prospective students and their parents. Wabash College, founded in 1832, references "men" only twice in its three-paragraph mission statement, and it does so only in passing, simply describing the college as "a liberal arts college for men" that offers "qualified young men a superior education, fostering, in particular independent intellectual inquiry, critical thought, and clear written oral and written expression." The college makes no link between this "superior" education and the absence of young women in its classes or campus life.[32]

Hampden-Sydney College, founded in 1732, references "men" only once in its mission statement, statement of purpose, and statement of core values, proclaiming that the college "seeks to form good men and good citizens in an atmosphere of sound learning."[33] In the absence of any sex-based claims, it seems then that the only justification for these colleges to continue their men-only admissions policies is tradition, but it is a quietly stated men-only tradition that avoids the unvarnished sexism spewed by VMI officials prior to the court-ordered demise of its male-only admissions policy.

Morehouse College, founded in 1867, differs from Wabash and Hampden-Sydney insofar as it describes itself as "a historically black liberal arts college for men" in its mission statement. Although the overwhelmingly majority of Morehouse students are African American men, the college, like any school receiving federal funds, cannot exclude prospective students from its admissions process on the basis of race. However, as a private college that was founded prior to 1972 and has been continuously single-sex since its founding, Morehouse is legally permitted under Title IX's exemption to bar women from its admissions process. Morehouse can and does market itself as assuming "special responsibility for teaching the history and culture of black people." But it cannot and does not formally market itself as a college "for black men," or a "black male college."

Like its historically and still predominately white counterparts, Wabash and Hampden-Sydney, Morehouse scarcely references sex classification in its mission statement, and draws no causal links between the quality of its education and the absence of female students on campus.[34] In 2010, Morehouse adopted a policy banning its students from wearing women's clothing on campus, but the policy was criticized for being homophobic rather than for being explicitly transphobic.[35]

Why Assimilation Won't Solve the Problem

One approach to solving the discriminatory impact of women-only college admissions on transgender women and men is to preserve the administrative requirement of being a woman and assimilate and/or accommodate transgender and gender-nonconforming prospective students into a more expansive definition of what that means.

Mount Holyoke has stretched its definition of "woman" the furthest of all its peer institutions. In 2015 the college amended its sex-based admissions policy to welcome "applications for our undergraduate program from any qualified student who is female or identifies as a woman."[36] But this prerequisite is contradicted by other information on its website, where the college lists the sex identities that are included in and excluded by its expanded definition of being female or identifying as a woman. According to this list, the only persons who are ineligible for admission under its new policy are people who were "biologically born male" and self-identify as men at the time of application.

Smith and Mills have stopped short of such elaboration, and now explicitly include self-defined transgender women as being eligible for admission, regardless of the sex markers that appear on their personal identity documents. Barnard College has changed its admissions policy to include "women who consistently live and identify as women, regardless of the gender assigned them at birth."[37] Bryn Mawr College now considers the eligibility of transgender women on a case-by-case basis based on legal sex documentation.[38] Wellesley College neither explicitly includes nor excludes transgender women in its admissions policies.[39]

Assimilation is arguably also the de facto approach of many nonelite women's colleges that have quietly admitted transgender women and men, and permitted students who transition from female to male post-enrollment to graduate on a case-by-case basis without making any formal changes to their admissions policies. Some women's colleges have ducked the issue of publicly stating whether or not they would admit a transgender woman or transgender man by simply stating that their admissions processes are open to "women" and/or "students who identify as female," without disclosing the criteria used for determining who meets these definitions.

These policies might be interpreted as being open to transgender women, gender-nonconforming people, as well as transgender men whose personal identity documents have female sex markers. But relying on "legal sex" is problematic because, as we saw in chapter 1, the criteria for changing the sex markers on particular legal identity documents such as birth certificates and driver's licenses differ from state to state. And even in cases where these documents bear a female sex marker, there may be other documentation in a person's file that describes the individual as male, such as a FAFSA form. This is precisely the problem that befell Calliope Wong when she applied to and was rejected by Smith.

Some women's colleges have focused their attention on less controversial changes to make their campuses more inclusive of matriculated transgender and gender-nonconforming students. For instance, many women's colleges have added the terms "gender identity" and/or "gender expression" to their nondiscrimination and diversity statements.[40] The provision of services and courses of study that include the term "transgender" might also be construed as signs of a school's acceptance of transgender students. The provision of gender-neutral or "all-gender" restrooms and the adjustment of campus housing policies to accommodate transgender and gender-nonconforming students could also be interpreted as indications that a college is open to transgender and gender-nonconforming applicants. Other key sex-classification policy nodes within colleges include student housing, name and sex marker changes in bureaucratic record keeping, and the use of gendered pronouns by faculty, staff, and students.

Many of these administrative changes are happening at elite liberal arts colleges. One reason for this is likely the presence of strong women's, gender, and sexuality studies academic departments, programs, and student centers. This is especially true at some of the nation's elite women's colleges, where feminist and gender scholars have often served on the committees charged with envisioning and structuring strategic initiatives and institutional change. It matters when students pushing for policy changes have the support of faculty, administrators, and alumni. But in the absence of any explicitly affirmative policies, it is difficult to gauge inclusiveness. It seems that many women's colleges are delaying taking an official stance on whether and how transgender students fit into their women-only admissions policies for as long as possible. When an institution adopts this kind of stance, it has decided to be reactive instead of taking the opportunity to be innovative and use the challenges posed by transgender identities to reevaluate its use of sex classification polices across the board.

None of the three private men's colleges has made any adjustments to its admissions policies to explicitly or implicitly assimilate transgender men or women into its institutional core values. This is likely due to the fact that there are so few men's colleges today, and those that remain are not considered as prestigious or elite as the Seven Sisters colleges. It also can be seen as further evidence of the trans-misogyny that Julia Serano describes as disproportionate fascination with and ridicule of transgender women in the media in comparison to transgender men.[41] Perhaps the prospect of a transgender man attending a men's college does not seem as titillating as a transgender woman attending a women's college.

Defining Sex and/or Gender

The women's colleges that have been forced or "peer-pressured" to publicly explain their women-only admissions policies express a political definition of "woman" and "female" that focuses on social construction rather than biology.

This differs markedly from many of the public arguments in favor of single-sex education at the K–12 level, which are largely based on claims that girls and boys have different learning needs and styles based on biological sex differences. Those arguments often invoke claims that girls and boys have different brains.[42] And when arguments are made about the distraction that the presence of girls poses for boys, there is a thinly veiled presumption that all children are heterosexual. In recent years, that debate has focused specifically on black boys and their putative need to be in all-black male schools with black male teachers to whom they can relate in an environment that is calibrated to their particular learning style. But as education scholar James Earl Davis points out, these kinds of schools do not empower all black boys; in fact such schools can marginalize and disempower boys whose gender expressions do not conform to hegemonic masculine standards.[43]

There may be some people affiliated with women's colleges who use biological, body-based arguments to defend sex segregation, but the official statements that appear on the websites of prominent women's colleges deliberately avoid essentialist claims that equate female identity and being a woman to physiology and hormones. Mount Holyoke's website, for instance, acknowledges important changes that have occurred in US feminism:

Just as early feminists argued that the reduction of women to their biological functions was a foundation for women's oppression, we must acknowledge that gender identity is not reducible to the body. Instead, we must look at identity in terms of the external context in which the individual is situated. It is this positionality that biological women and transwomen share, and it is this positionality that is relevant when women's colleges open their gates for those aspiring to live, learn, and thrive within a community of women.[44]

Mount Holyoke's stress on the "external context" of women's "positionality" is reminiscent of the political theorist Iris Marion Young's compelling argument that women are more accurately theorized as a "series" than as an "identity group." Intersecting identities such as race and class mean that there are multiple experiences and self-identities among women. They are not a group, which Young defines as a collection of individuals with common interests and attitudes, in the way that, for example, the National Rifle Association and the Daughters of the Confederacy are groups. Instead, she describes women as a series, meaning that they are drawn together by the experience of having to deal with the common political problem of sexism.[45] Being a woman does not predetermine one's political beliefs about what this sexism entails and how it should be addressed.

Mount Holyoke does not explain what it means by "women's positionality." The college asserts a commonality between cisgender and transgender women, but does not explain what exactly these women have in common. If it is the sort of seriality invoked by Young, does it matter that some transgender women will have been socialized as boys and/or men for certain periods of their lives?

Transgender men are mentioned in the "frequently asked questions" section of the policy. But Mount Holyoke's policy statement makes no mention of them. There seems to be an underlying presumption that transgender men should be included because they have been socialized as girls and/or women, and therefore belong to the series of women. But is socialization the same thing as positionality? As previously discussed, many variables come into play, such as the age at which the person transitioned from female to male, and whether the person is gender-conforming or gender-nonconforming in her or his (or their) self-identification and how he or she (or they) appears to other people in particular contexts.

Ginsburg's focus on "artificial constraint" and statistical sex-role stereotypes can shed light on the ways that single-sex admissions policies, even those as flexible and expansive as Mount Holyoke's, can and often do produce sex-based exclusion. The burden should be on the college to prove that the exclusion of biologically born men who identify as men at the time of their application is necessary for the college to carry out its mission of creating an institutional space for its students "to live, learn, and thrive within a community of women." It seems likely that many, and perhaps most, men would not seek the kind of education offered by women's colleges. But some men might seek such an education and may personally benefit from being in such a learning environment. Women, too, might benefit from being in a female-dominant institution with men. Women's colleges can and should continue to follow their core values and missions. But these legitimate policy goals should be pursued via other means than the continuance of single-sex admissions.

Mount Holyoke went through an important iterative process of explicitly enumerating all the sex-identity groups that may apply for admission. These include "biologically born" females who identify as women, men, other/they/ze, or do not identify as either women or men; "biologically born" males who identify as female, or other/they/ze when "other/they" means self-identification as a woman; or persons who are "biologically born" with male and female anatomy (intersex) and identify as women.[46] Perhaps the exclusion of "biologically born males" who self-identify as men at the time of their application is needed in order for Mount Holyoke to market itself as a "women's college." But is that really true?

As a practical matter, Mount Holyoke's antiessentialist definition of what it means to self-identify as female or a woman is undermined by the way it asks prospective students to record their sex-identities on its application forms. When an application form prompts a prospective student to check a male or female box, what definition of sex identity is the person being asked to disclose? Is it a first-person self-understanding of being a male or being a female? Or is it a third-person perception of how others may perceive the person in relation to the social and legal scheme of binary sex? What should an applicant do when these two conceptions diverge? What about the person who wants to check both male and female boxes, or neither?

On the Common Application, which is used by over six hundred colleges, including Mount Holyoke, a sex classification question appears on the first screen after the user creates a password for the website. The applicant must select either male or female in order to progress to the rest of the application. When I accessed the form in January 2016, to the right of this binary sex question an information icon appeared. When clicked, the following notice appeared:

> Federal guidelines mandate that we collect data on the *legal sex* of all applicants.
>
> Please report the sex currently listed on your *birth certificate*. If you wish to provide more details regarding your gender identity, you are welcome to do so in the additional information section.[47]

The informational note recognized that a person's birth sex designation does not always match the person's sex identity over the course of a lifetime, or more pointedly, at the time of application. When I accessed the Common Application in October 2016, the informational note had been removed. Applicants were now prompted to check a male or female option as their "sex assigned at birth." The next prompt read, "If you would like the opportunity, we invite you to share more about your gender identity below." The invitation to provide further information is a nod to the fact that sex identity can be more complex.

Nevertheless, the mandatory prompt to disclose the sex that appears on our birth certificates is deeply problematic. As discussed in chapter 2, the sex markers on our birth certificate are based upon a physician's visual inspection of our external genitalia at birth.[48] Also, the requirements for changing birth certificate sex markers vary across states, and can be cumbersome and difficult. In the state of Tennessee such an amendment is legally impossible, so transgender people born in Tennessee cannot legally align their lived sex identity with their legal sex documentation. Many transgender people have changed some of their identity documents, but not all. So, an applicant might have a driver's license with a female sex marker and a birth certificate with a male sex marker.

Sex-classification questions on college application forms presume a fixed and verifiable definition of binary sex identity that fails to take into account transgender and gender-nonconforming experience. These experiences tell us that the sex classifications assigned to us at birth are changeable over the course of our lifetimes. The ubiquity of male/female bureaucratic box checking can make this action seem trivial and apolitical. Indeed, most often sex-identity questions appear near the beginning of the bureaucratic form, as if it is a preliminary matter of course, equally as necessary as our name and address.

But sex identity is neither straightforward nor easy for everyone faced with college forms, and checking a male or female box can mean outright exclusion from a particular educational opportunity. And in other cases, it is unclear how a particular institution or organization will use this information. No men's colleges have taken steps to define "men" in their mission statements or explanation of their admissions process.

"Choice Architecture"

Women's colleges have a long history of creating higher education environments that are designed to fight institutional sexism. When women were barred from applying to many colleges, this fight meant providing parallel institutions for women. Today, institutional sexism persists, and women's colleges have a vital leadership role to play in paving the way for other colleges to do things differently.

But single-sex admissions are not necessary for doing this critical work. The increased visibility of transgender and gender-nonconforming identities is an opportunity for these schools to consider in a more focused way the relationship between the collection of sex-identity information and their educational mission. An important place to begin this institutional self-reflection and reform is the sex classification questions that appear on college application forms.

The idea of "choice architecture" can help administrative policy makers take up this work. In their popular book *Nudge*, legal scholar Cass Sunstein and economist Richard Thaler introduce this term.[49] They argue that we are prompted or nudged to make certain choices based upon how those choices are physically presented to us. Consider for example the common practice used in many stores of stocking small sugary snacks at eye level near cash registers. We are visually prompted but not forced to purchase these items while we wait in line to pay for the things already in our carts or baskets. Sunstein and Thaler recommend rearranging this choice architecture so that we are nudged to make healthier food choices in a supermarket. They base this principle on the political theory concept of limited paternalism elaborated by the liberal political philosopher John Stuart Mill in his classic essay "On Liberty."[50]

Political theorists Elizabeth Markovits and Susan Bickford apply the idea of choice architecture to feminism. In the supermarket example, the idea was to promote the good of healthier eating. In the context of feminism and the US workplace, Markovits and Bickford propose redesigning the bureaucratic "choice architecture" of human resource paperwork so that individuals are nudged to make choices that promote gender equality. They suggest reconfiguring W-4 forms to give workers the choice of having their paycheck divided between them and a designated partner, or paid fully to them. The important nudge in this example is that the option of splitting the person's salary between the worker and the spouse or partner is the default option. To have the full payment go to the employee, the individual must actively make a different choice.[51]

This reform retains Mill's limited paternalism because it nudges but does not force an individual to make the feminist choice.

Policy Redesign

My recommendation is that women-only and men-only colleges open their admissions processes to everyone. At the same time, I think it's very important that historically women's colleges retain their feminist mission, and that historically men's colleges, and indeed all colleges, adopt such a mission.

Figuring out how to do this will require more work on the part of college administrators. Or, perhaps a better way to phrase it is that administrators will need to have a different, more focused conversation about ends and means. A literal and pragmatic interpretation of the legal rational relationship test can light the way. One strategy would be for college administrators to use a feminist choice architecture to collect and process sex-identity information from prospective students that is closely tied to their educational goals of diversity.

Colleges might, for example, make the sex-identity questions on their application forms voluntary instead of mandatory. This would mean treating sex like race, which colleges are permitted to ask but cannot require of applicants. Application form designers should not stop there. In asking for information about a candidate's sex, colleges should explain what definition of sex and/or gender they are invoking. Are they interested in knowing how the candidate self-identifies in relation to these concepts, and/or the person's assessment of her or his third-person race-sex identification, how others see the individual?

Colleges could ask prospective students to reflect upon how their own sex identities relate to the college's commitment to fighting institutional sexism. This information could be conveyed in a short essay and/or in the personal interviews that many elite colleges use in their recruitment processes. In the revised choice architecture of sex-identity questioning, some discussion about cisgender men could be helpful. How might the presence of these students help further the college's feminist mission? What are some of the ways that their presence can threaten and undermine this legitimate and important mission? What assumptions are being made about this sex-identity group?

Colleges might add an informational note to their sex-identity question(s) that explicitly notes the temporal nature of such questions. Here is an excellent opportunity for a school to acknowledge that a person's sex classification can change over time. There is also the question of what, if anything, a women's college should do when a matriculated student begins or continues a sex-identity transition after matriculation or graduation. Some students who do transition during their college years face difficulties in having their felt sex identities bureaucratically validated. For instance, their diplomas may or may not display their post-transition name. Moreover, some transgender men who do not wish to be out as transgender can face awkward situations when potential employers see a women's college on their transcript or resume.

Sex-identity questionnaires envelop many of the other sex-classification policies discussed in this book. When and how do colleges, both single-sex and coed, use sex-marked government identity documents? How does the presence of transgender women and men and gender-nonconforming students affect the administration of sex-segregated restrooms on campus, as well as student dormitories and locker rooms for athletics? What are the implications of single-sex colleges for questions about sex-segregated sports? To what extent should sex classification be taken into account when it comes to recruiting, hiring, and promoting faculty and staff at both single-sex and coed colleges?

Conclusion

Our sex identities are relevant to the diversity goals of colleges, but their institutional relevance should be explained by particular colleges, rather than assumed.

The reason for doing so, to be clear, is not because sex identity is unimportant. On the contrary, it is because our right to say who we are in relationship to the social and legal scheme of binary sex is so important to us that we should take great care to minimize the institutional opportunities for administrative processes and agents to evaluate this aspect of our lives and possibly overrule our sex-identity self-statements.

4

Seeing Sex in the Body

Sex-Segregated Sports

In 2009, Caster Semenya, an eighteen-year-old black South African track star, became the subject of an international sex-identity scandal. Semenya self-identifies as female, and has for her entire life. Yet, rumors had been brewing in the track-and-field world for years that she was a man. She was accused of being too masculine to compete as female after winning the gold medal and breaking the world record in the women's eight-hundred-meter race at the Berlin World Championships in Athletics.

A leaked fax to the press indicated that the International Association of Athletics Federations (IAAF) had already subjected Semenya to "sex-testing" before the race. The leak claimed that the results of that testing showed that Semenya had an intersex condition called hyperandrogenism. People with this condition are born with XX chromosomes, but they produce androgens at three times the levels of typical females. Reportedly, Semenya had been subjected to a two-hour medical examination during which her genitalia were visually inspected and photographed. The report indicated that she had undescended testes and no uterus. She was not informed that she was being tested for her sex identity. Instead, she was told that she was going through a routine test for performance-enhancing drugs.

The official results of her sex-verification test have never been publicly confirmed. But that didn't matter because she had already been tried and found guilty in the court of public opinion based upon her physical appearance. Ariel Levy, writing for the *New Yorker*, described her as "breathtakingly butch" and depicted Semenya's body in vivid detail. "Her torso is like the chest plate on a suit of armor. She has a strong jawline, and a build that slides straight down from her ribs to her hips."[1]

Many of Semenya's competitors pointed to her masculine appearance as the reason for their losses to her on the track. Elise Cusma, an Italian runner who finished in sixth place at the 2009 World Championships, told the press, "These kind of people should not run with us. For me, she is not a woman. She is a man." And Mariya Savinova of Russia, who placed fifth in the race, said it all without saying anything: "Just look at her." The allegations came so frequently that Semenya got used to her competitors asking to see her genitals as proof that she was female. For whatever reasons, she often obliged. "They are doubting me," Semenya would tell her coaches, "as she headed off the field to the lavatory" to be inspected.[2] Allegedly, she was "really" a man pretending to be a woman in order to win gold medals and set world records at any cost. But in reality she was just too strong and too fast for women's track and field.

Suspicion that Semenya's strong physique was the result of performance-enhancing drugs would not be unusual. In elite competition where money and glory are at stake, both male and female athletes must routinely undergo testing for banned substances in nearly every elite sports competition. Most people accept such testing as rationally related to the legitimate policy goal of deterring and catching cheaters. At the same time, most experts concede that it is practically impossible for the testing of banned substances to keep up with new doping techniques that are always at least one step ahead of the techniques for detecting them.[3] But female athletes who appear to be extremely muscular *and* are competitively dominant are vulnerable to the further suspicion and accusation that they are "really men" or are "trying to be men."

These allegations are often intertwined with racism and homophobia.[4] Black female athletes who are muscular, dark-skinned, and competitively dominant such as Semenya have historically been and continue to be stereotyped as masculine and ugly, and thus failing to measure up to hegemonic feminine standards of being the kind of woman that straight men sexually desire. Elite white female tennis players who are muscular such as Sam Stosur and former players Amélie Mauresmo and Martina Navratilova have all been ridiculed for "looking manly." Serena and Venus Williams have been derided as too masculine, but they have also been called gorillas and apes.[5] In 2014 the president of the Russian Tennis Federation, Shamil Tarpischev, publicly described the sisters as "brothers" who are "scary" to look at.[6] The allegation was not sincere. Tarpischev was not implying that the Williams sisters are female impersonators—men who dress up in female garb to play tennis. Instead, he meant to discredit their unprecedented success by publicly shaming and humiliating them.

Rarely do such statements lead to the kind of physical inspection that Semenya endured. However, if the evidence of our sex identity lies in our bodies, as most people believe it does, then some kind of inspection of this evidence seems necessary for upholding all forms of sex segregation. Our bodies are directly involved in sports. For this reason, the sports world brings us face-to-face with the physical dimensions of sex identity in a way that the other case studies in this book do not. The shape, size, and endocrinology of our bodies matter for sports because changing these features can alter our physical strength and stamina, both of which can bestow competitive advantage. Even so, it is crucial to note that a lot of other factors, such as the genetic gifts we are born with as well as our personal motivation, training, and even luck, go into becoming a competitively dominant athlete. Moreover, athletic success is not just about winning. Many people seek other ends in sport, such as camaraderie, self-discipline, recreation, and fun. How does sex identity relate to these and other sports-related goals?

The most common defense of sex segregation in sports is "fair play." But this term is a Trojan horse for a host of more specific goals that we, as a society, seek in sport. Among these goals are equal opportunity, the spectacle of gendered and racialized bodies, student athleticism, and recreation. Is sex segregation rationally related to all of these goals? I believe that sex is related to some, but not all, of these objectives. Age and the level of play matter greatly for whether and how sex identity is relevant in sports. Only when we bring these factors into focus will we be in a good position to make recommendations about which sports-related sex-classification policies might be eliminated, and which might be retained and perhaps revised.

What's the Harm?

In my view, sex segregation in sports generates three kinds of sexism.

The first can be described as "tyranny of the majority," whereby the minority of transgender, intersex, and gender-nonconforming individuals are singled out for invasive sex-identity questioning and inspection that can disqualify them from participating in sports. As previously discussed, sex-identity discrimination disproportionately impacts people who are perceived by others to have changed or to be in the process of changing their birth sex designation, as well as those who are perceived to have a combination of male and female bodily characteristics. The direct harms of harassment and exclusion subsume the indirect but serious harm of stifling and thwarting the athletic ambitions of people who fear being subjected to such questioning and exclusion in either the short or long term. Imagine the chilling effect that Semenya's ordeal has had on intersex and transgender youth throughout the world who otherwise may have pursued their Olympic dreams in track and field and other sex-segregated sports.

The second harm caused by sex-segregated sports policies is the more familiar sexism of sex-based disadvantage, whereby girls and women incur a disadvantage in relationship to men, and in some cases men incur a disadvantage in relationship to women. Unequal funding, financial rewards, equipment, and social prestige exemplify such disadvantage. A case in point is the federal wage discrimination complaint that five members of the US women's national soccer team have filed with the Equal Employment Opportunity Commission. The women are paid as little as 40 percent of the US men's national soccer team wages. The gap is especially glaring in light of the fact that the women's national team has won three world and four Olympic championships, whereas the men's team has no such victories to its name.[7]

Elite female soccer players have also had to contend with inferior playing conditions. After it was announced that the 2015 FIFA Women's World Cup tournament in Canada would be played on artificial turf instead of grass, a group of eighty female players from various national teams filed a gender discrimination lawsuit against FIFA and the Canadian Soccer Association, which was later withdrawn. Artificial turf causes intense heat radiation of up to 120 degrees Fahrenheit, increases rates of injury, and causes unpredictable ball bounces.[8] The men's FIFA tournament has never been played on artificial turf. This is the "separate and unequal" problem that accompanies most forms of sex segregation.

As with sex-segregated public restrooms, with athletics it is difficult and often impossible to establish and maintain substantive equality between sex-segregated facilities and/or programs for three main reasons. First, there is disagreement over the criteria for measuring and monitoring equality. We saw this problem in the so-called "potty parity" lawsuits in chapter 2, and we see it again in Title IX litigation in which the measure of gender parity in school sports has shifted over time.

Second, in modeling the parallel facility or program after the existing facility or program, policy makers fail to address the sexism of the model facility or program. For instance, just as women's restrooms are modified versions of men's restrooms (i.e., without urinals), the Women's National Basketball Association (WNBA) and Ladies Professional Golfers' Association (LPGA) are modified versions of the National Basketball Association (NBA) and Professional Golfers' Association (PGA). In none of these cases was the original men's version of a restroom, basketball, or golf game modified.

Third, sex segregation in sports harms all of us by constricting our capacity to say where and with whom we belong in the social scheme of sex. Sports function as an important social institution for the reproduction and reinforcement of binary norms concerning masculinity and femininity that affect all of us—whether we are athletes, spectators, or neither. We receive these messages very early on in our lives, as most boys are steered toward aggressive sports and most girls are steered away from such play. Body-based sex-verification policies at elite levels of sports send a strong message to all of us that sex identity is supposed to be visually obvious and stable over time. They also tell us that the policing of female masculinity is an important, if not the *most* important means of ensuring "a level playing field."

Looking for Sex in the Body

What happened to Semenya was a violation of the IAAF's current policies, which ban sex testing, but it was not unprecedented in the world of elite international athletic competition.

The International Olympic Committee (IOC) instituted its first physical sex-verification policy at the 1968 Mexico City Summer Games. Athletes wishing to compete as female were subjected to genital inspection. This invasive practice sometimes meant standing or walking naked in front of a panel of "experts." This came to be called the "nude parade." At other times, it required women to lie down naked on a table and pull their knees to their chest to allow examiners to more closely inspect their genitals.

Not surprisingly, this sex verification practice elicited numerous complaints. The IOC subsequently adopted what became known as the Barr body test to verify that all female athletes had XX chromosomes. The IOC designated "experts" to collect mouth swabs from each athlete wishing to compete as female. Anyone whose buccal smear test yielded anything other than an XX chromosomal makeup was barred from competing as a woman in the Olympic Games.[9]

Ostensibly these measures were intended to detect and deter men from posing as women for the purpose of gaining competitive advantage. In the heat of the Cold War, Olympic competition reflected the bitter and protracted rivalry between the "free" Western world and the closed societies ruled by dictators behind the Iron Curtain of the Soviet Bloc. Within this environment of "good" versus "evil," the prospect of

the communists cheating by any means, including female imperson-
ation, may have seemed like a legitimate threat.

It has now been documented that the Soviet Union ran an extensive
program of administering massive quantities of performance-enhancing
drugs to athletes. Many of those drugs were androgens, which had masculinizing effects on the appearances of many Soviet female swimmers,
weight lifters, and track-and-field athletes. What I find morally wrong
about this widespread doping is the lack of informed consent among
athletes, not the "masculinizing" effects of androgens such as testosterone on female athletes.[10] Many athletes in the "free world" were using
steroids as well, and in most cases they were doing so of their own voli-
tion, in the absence of government coercion.

For the 2012 London Summer Games, the IOC dropped the language
of sex testing from its policies. Since then, any athlete wishing to compete as female must be tested for the levels of "functional" testosterone that her body both makes and responds to before being registered
to compete as female in an Olympic event. The distinction between
"makes" and "responds to" is important because some intersex women
have undescended testes that produce a lot of testosterone, but their
bodies do not respond to that androgen—an intersex condition called
androgen insensitivity syndrome (AIS). People with AIS appear to be
typical girls and women, but they have male chromosomes.[11]

The Spanish former elite hurdler Maria Martínez-Patiño found out
that she had AIS after she failed a chromosome test at the 1985 World
University Games in Kobe, Japan. She had forgotten to bring her "certificate of femininity" with her. When that happened, the policy at the
time required the athlete to undergo a chromosome test at the event.
Cells scraped from Martínez-Patiño's inner cheek revealed that she had
a Y chromosome. In consequence of failing the sex test she was stripped
of her past titles, lost her scholarship, and was evicted from the national
athletic residence.[12]

The testing for functional testosterone is in addition to the standard testing of all athletes for performance-enhancing drugs. Not all

performance-enhancing drugs are androgens. At the 2015 Australian Open the elite female tennis player Maria Sharapova tested positive for the banned drug meldonium and was suspended. Meldonium purportedly increases an athlete's cardiovascular capacity, but does not alter an athlete's physiological appearance.[13] According to the IOC's policy, if an athlete's functional testosterone levels fall within the normal range of testosterone for males, then the athlete may not compete as female, but may compete as male.

But there is a lapse in the logic here that simmers beneath a cover of hypocrisy. Under this policy testosterone is used as the proxy for female ineligibility, which effectively makes it the test for "being" a man, at least for the purpose of sex-segregated Olympic competition. But there has never been a corresponding test for athletes wishing to compete as male. This means that it is possible for a female person to compete as male, thereby technically violating the IOC's sex-segregation policies. However, a man whose testosterone levels fall below the normal range for males may not cross the binary sex line to compete as female.

The IOC's policies are important because they set a kind of "best practices" standard for how other elite sports-governing bodies administrate sex identity. Following the lead of the IOC, the National Collegiate Athletic Association (NCAA) currently uses testosterone measurement to determine sex-specific eligibility in elite Division I college sports such as football, basketball, and track and field. But unlike the IOC, the NCAA does not administer such testing itself.[14] The NCAA bans the use of testosterone because of its performance-enhancing effects.

Therefore, transgender male athletes who are currently using or planning to use testosterone as part of their sex-identity transition must submit a written request for a "medical exception" to the director of athletics at their school. The students must also obtain and submit a letter from a physician that verifies that the testosterone is being prescribed for the treatment of "diagnosed Gender Identity Disorder or gender dysphoria and/or Transsexualism." The director of athletics must then notify the

NCAA of the students' medical exception request.[15] This is reminiscent of the federal government and some state governments' requirement that transgender people present a letter from a physician attesting to the permanence or sincerity of a person's request to change the sex markers on personal identity documents.

In 2010, Kye Allums made headlines for being the first publicly self-identified transgender man to play on a Division I NCAA women's basketball team. Allums came out to his coach and teammates in his junior year, and was allowed to continue to play for the George Washington University women's basketball team because he had not begun testosterone therapy.[16] A transgender male athlete who has not used and is not planning to use testosterone may compete as either male or female. A transgender male athlete who is using or planning to use testosterone and has obtained a medical exception may compete as male, but may not compete as female.

By sexist contrast, a transgender female student who is using or is planning to use testosterone-suppressing medication for medically diagnosed gender identity disorder or gender dysphoria and/or transsexualism may compete as male but not female. A transgender female student-athlete who is not using any hormone treatments for her sex-identity transition may not compete as a female.[17]

The NCAA has adopted a confusing set of policies that allow men and women to play on opposite-gender teams, while simultaneously barring particular gender "mixtures" from intercollegiate competition. In 2006, the NCAA added the category of "mixed team" to its bylaws: "A mixed team is a varsity intercollegiate sports team on which at least one individual of each gender competes." This means that, formally speaking, men can play on women's teams and women can play on men's teams. However, once a man has joined a female team, that team becomes a mixed team that is ineligible for a female NCAA championship, but eligible for a male NCAA championship. By sexist contrast, once a female joins a male team that team becomes a mixed team but remains eligible for a male NCAA championship.[18]

The NCAA's sex-verification policy is based upon a mixture of self-reporting, medical documentation, and athletic directors' due diligence. There have been no publicized allegations of men "impersonating" women in order to seek competitive advantage within sex-segregated sports, and the NCAA has never stated this as the justification for its current policy. Like the IOC's testosterone test, the NCAA's policy purports to be general, but in practice it singles out and disqualifies certain intersex and transgender athletes.

Because the policy provides no way for a transgender woman to participate in NCAA competition *as female*, it also exemplifies "trans misogyny." This kind of misogyny is an extension of the general assumption that "femaleness and femininity are inferior to, and exist primarily for the benefit of, maleness and masculinity." Transgender and non-transgender women both experience the "cultural assumption that a woman's power and worth stems primarily from her ability to be sexualized by others." But, as previously discussed, transgender women incur the additional sexism of being culturally portrayed as sexual deceivers who are out to trick heterosexual men into having sex with them.[19]

This trans misogyny seeps into the world of sport, where the deception is not explicitly about sexual activity, but more about who wins and loses. The connection between testosterone and sex classification is not as simple or straightforward as the IOC's and NCAA's policies imply. I would posit that our sex identities are not reducible to the amount of testosterone we have in our bloodstream at a given time. If testosterone measures were truly dispositive of binary sex classification, then testing Semenya's blood for her functional testosterone levels would have solved the "mystery" of her sex identity. But the hunt for her "real" sex identity continued. Her genitals were inspected and photographed.

And even that wasn't enough, so the hunt continued inside her body for information about her reproductive organs. And just as testosterone levels, alone, do not make us men or women, they are not the sole predictor of who wins and loses in sports. If that were the case, then there would be no need to hold track meets and tournaments; we could pick winners by measuring whose body makes and responds to the greatest amount of functional testosterone. Fortunately, many other factors such as sport-specific skills, training, and luck factor into athletic performance.

All that said, it is undeniable that hormones cause major physiological changes in our bodies, and that these changes send visual cues to others about our maleness or femaleness. This is precisely why hormone therapy is an important aspect of sex-identity transition for many, though not all, transgender people. Testosterone and estrogen therapies are used to alter some of the mutable physical characteristics we associate with being a male and being a female. Some transgender men use testosterone therapy to achieve secondary male sex characteristics such as facial hair, a deeper voice, and changes in the bodily distribution of fat and muscle.

Some also undergo surgical procedures such as a bilateral mastectomy to remove breast tissue. Genital surgery is less common among transgender men than "top surgery," but some choose to undergo surgeries such as phalloplasty and metoidioplasty. Some transgender women use estrogen therapy to achieve some of the secondary sex characteristics associated with female sex identity, such as increased ratio of fat to muscle, and the production of breast tissue. Some also choose to undergo surgical procedures such as the shaving down of a pronounced Adam's apple, breast implants, facial feminization surgeries, and genital surgery.[20]

Many of these bodily changes, such as the presence of an Adam's apple, facial bone structure, the ability to grow a beard, and the shape, size, and functionality of genitalia and internal reproductive organs, are irrelevant to athletic performance. (Some transgender men undergo partial or full hysterectomies, but many do not.) But other changes pertaining to musculature and the production of red blood cells that affect lung capacity do affect our athletic capacity and thus our competitiveness.

When I began using testosterone therapy as part of my transition from female to male at the age of thirty-eight, I felt somewhat bionic. I noticed that I was able to run faster and for longer periods of time. But

I was very far from setting any records, even for my age group! How should the administration of sex-segregated sports change in light of these possibilities that are not new, but are now being publicly acknowledged and discussed?

Fair Play

Many people have never seriously questioned sex segregation in sports because they assume it is necessary for achieving fair play. Indeed, this wisdom is so conventional that the comedian Chris Rock spun one of his best jokes around it when he hosted the 2016 Academy Awards. In castigating the sex-segregated categories of "best actor" and "best actress" as sexist, Rock fired off, "This isn't track and field. It's not like Robert De Niro is 'like, I need to slow down so Meryl Streep can catch up.'" The Academy of Motion Pictures should get rid of its sex-segregated acting award categories. But the need for sex segregation in track and field and other sports is not as obvious and straightforward as Rock's zinger implies.

Equal Opportunity

One definition of fairness is equal opportunity. When we speak of equal opportunity in sports, we typically have in mind the formal equality that the nineteenth-century English philosopher John Stuart Mill describes in his essay *The Subjection of Women*. Mill does not discuss athletic competition, but he makes the classical liberal argument that competitions for social goods such as employment and education should be open to individual men and women, regardless of their sex identity.[21] This is the sex-blind version of fairness. When the doors are flung open and all are allowed to compete, Mill, along with his contemporary libertarian adherents, argues that the best person(s) will win.

Libertarians endorse a conception of justice that is outcome-indifferent, meaning that any pattern of winners and losers is acceptable so long as everyone was allowed to compete for the social good. This conception of equality has deep hooks in American culture, even among self-described progressives. If I had a nickel for every time I heard a colleague describe a faculty job search as a quest to find the best "athlete" I would have a full piggy bank by now. When the best people win the social goods at stake, Mill and many of my colleagues believe that we boost the overall social utility or welfare of organizations and the greater society.

Applied to the actual world of sports, formal equality typically means that individuals should not be prevented from trying out for a competitive sports team, or entering an individual athletic competition because of their sex. But even the most diehard libertarians do not believe that we should ignore sex and age in athletic competition. We use age as a proxy for certain ranges of physical size and strength. It seems patently unfair to pit a five-year-old kid against an eighteen-year-old adolescent, or a thirty-five-year-old adult against a seventy-five-year-old adult.

If men and women compete against one another in sports that require brawn and speed, there is a legitimate concern that boys and men will be winners most of the time, and that girls and women will be losers most of the time. This is because *most* boys and men are bigger and physically stronger than most girls and women.

This statistical fact spawns the worry that girls and women will incur physical injury at higher rates than boys and men in sports involving physical contact such as football and ice hockey.

This fear is reminiscent of the "man in the women's bathroom" panic discussed earlier.[22] In sports, there is an analogous stereotype of the man who infiltrates women's athletic competition. In the bathroom scenario, the claim is that if sex-segregated restrooms are not maintained, then men will enter women's restrooms to ogle and physically assault them. In the sports arena, the claim is that if sex segregation is not maintained, then girls and women will be physically harmed. This paternalism, or what some people describe as "benevolent sexism" (sexism that aims to help rather than hinder women), interfaces with the policing of female masculinity. When female athletes are extremely muscular and competitively dominant, they are often accused of harming other female players. This happens in female-designated sports even when there is no physical contact. Recall the Russian Tennis Federation president's comment that Serena Williams is "scary to look at."

On closer inspection, the protection of female athletes via paternalistic policies is not as "rational" as it may seem. Such policies are "overbroad" because they do not account for the substantial intrasexual variation in musculature, bone density, lung capacity, stature, and endocrinology that exists within the categories of people we call male and female. There are plenty of big and strong women, and plenty of small and weak men. Moreover, mounting scientific evidence regarding the deleterious short- and long-term effects of concussions on football and hockey players should make us question whether the norms of these hypermasculine sports should be changed. For instance, is periodic fist fighting truly integral to professional men's ice hockey? Or would we all be better off without it?

Assimilation

When it comes to sports, mainstream liberal feminists have interpreted the concept of equal opportunity as a two-tiered process of assimilation and accommodation within the structure of sex-segregated sports. In the 1970s, the women's liberation movement focused on assimilating individual female athletes into male-only teams and competition. The success of this strategy led to the creation of several girls' and women's parallel sports leagues and events. Later, many of the feminists who had fought for the integration of previously all-male teams switched their focus to an accommodation approach of making separate female-designated sports substantively equal to their male-designated counterparts. Too much was conceded in this switch, as I explain below.

In 1972, the assimilation strategists won a major legal victory in the case of Maria Pepe, a thirteen-year-old star pitcher from New Jersey who wanted to play on her local Little League baseball team.[23] The league coordinators denied Pepe's application, citing Little League's official regulations at the time explicitly stating that "girls are ineligible." The organization added this statement to its federal charter in 1950 in response to pressure from other girls who wished to join their local teams.[24] By the time of Pepe's legal challenge, Little League had successfully defended itself against two other sex-discrimination lawsuits.

The plaintiffs in those cases argued that the organization's federal charter effectively made it a "state actor" beholden to the Fourteenth Amendment's Equal Protection Clause barring any state from denying "any person within its jurisdiction the equal protection of the laws." But federal courts rejected that premise and dismissed both cases. Pepe and her parents, along with their National Organization for Women legal counsel, ultimately won their case by framing her exclusion as a violation of New Jersey's civil rights code barring sex discrimination in public accommodations. Little League is a private corporation, but the fact that its member state franchises used and continue to use public parks and playing fields for their practices and games means that it must follow state laws that bar sex discrimination in public accommodations.[25]

Subsequent state court rulings extended the definition of a public accommodation to include privately owned and city-owned municipal parks.[26] And in 1992, an Arizona state court ruled that *federal* public accommodations nondiscrimination laws also apply to Little League.[27] In 2000, a federal court further ruled that sporting leagues themselves are public accommodations.[28] Based upon these rulings, other sports organizations that use public accommodations for their activities are susceptible to civil rights lawsuits on similar grounds. Furthermore, it would seem that state and municipal ordinances that bar discrimination in public accommodations on the basis of gender identity and/or gender expression would also apply to sports leagues and organizations, although no such lawsuits, to my knowledge, have been filed.

The public accommodations legal framework has also been used to assimilate transgender women into some female-only athletic competitions. In 1976, Renée Richards, a white transgender woman, used New York State's Human Rights Law banning gender discrimination in public accommodations to successfully sue the United States Tennis Association (USTA). The USTA had refused to register her for the ladies' draw of the US Open, a major professional tournament that takes place every August and September in Flushing Meadows, Queens, unless she submitted to a medical test proving that she was "born female." Prior to her sex-identity transition, Richards had been highly ranked in men's college tennis, playing for Yale. Post-transition, Richards was moderately successful. She reached her highest ranking of twentieth in 1979, and retired from professional tennis in 1981 at the age of forty-seven.

In a surprising turn of events, Richards, who became a renowned eye surgeon, now believes that transgender women should not be allowed to compete as women in elite sports because of their physiological competitive advantage. As she states, "There is one thing that a transsexual woman cannot expect to be allowed to do, and that is to play professional sports in her chosen field. She can get married, live as a woman, do all of those other things, and no one should ever be allowed to take them away from her. But this limitation—that's just life. I know because I lived it."[29]

Other transgender women disagree and are seeking inclusion in women's athletic competition. In 2010, Lana Lawless, a white transgender woman, used California's civil rights law banning gender identity discrimination in public accommodations to sue the LPGA, the World Long-Drive Association, and two LPGA corporate sponsors. At the time, the LPGA had an official policy that required all female players to be "women born women."[30] Of course the phrase "women born women" really means "women born girls" since none of us are born adults.

Lawless did not experience the invasive and illegal physical inspection that Semenya endured. Nevertheless, the term "women born women" invokes the genital inspection that all of us underwent at birth and perhaps prior to birth on the ultrasound monitor screen. So when we are asked for our "birth sex," there is a presumption both that the delivering physician's judgment constitutes our true and objective sex identity and that such a true and objective sex identity cannot "really" be changed. Yet, as previously discussed, most states permit transgender people to change the sex marker on their birth certificate as long as they are able to produce medical documentation of a sex-identity change, so how stable is this measure of sex?

Shortly after Lawless filed her lawsuit, the LPGA players association voted to remove the "women born women" policy from its constitution. As of this writing, the LPGA has not instituted new language regarding sex verification. Neither the USTA nor the PGA has ever instituted an analogous "men born men" membership policy. The organization appears to be taking an approach similar to many women's colleges that have not been dragged into the public spotlight: treating the assimilation of transgender female golfers on a case-by-case basis. This is a reactive, rather than proactive, way of reforming the administration of sex. The public accommodation legal strategy does not apply to private clubs that are open only to members and do not use public facilities or private facilities that are open to the public. Such organizations are legally free to discriminate on the basis of sex and race, as well as any other attribute.[31]

In the summer of 2014, a thirteen-year-old African American pitcher named Mo'ne Davis made the cover of *Sports Illustrated* for leading her all-male Philadelphia Little League baseball team to the League's World Series held in Williamsport, Pennsylvania. I cheered her along with just about everyone else in the Philadelphia area, and many other fans across the country. Yet, it was striking to see a lone girl on an all-male team some forty years after Maria Pepe, also a star pitcher at thirteen, had broken down the legal barrier to girls playing in Little League.

The late 1970s also saw a number of previously all-boys youth hockey, soccer, basketball, and football leagues open their doors to girls. But in most cases, there was just one girl "integrating" the team, and she was provided with a separate place to change into her equipment. Why are there so few girls playing Little League baseball today? The Little League Association, a nonprofit national outfit that issues charters to individual states, was court-ordered to open its doors to girls in 1974. But shortly thereafter it invented a parallel "girls" softball league, which effectively subverted girls' demand for "baseball" by creating a new demand for the new game of "softball," which was heavily marketed to girls and their parents.[32]

Accommodation

Many youth leagues eventually created separate girls' hockey, soccer, and lacrosse teams. In the 1990s, girls' soccer and hockey were the fastest growing youth sports in the United States. At the same time, major league sports began creating nominal women's leagues in their own efforts to subvert female demand for inclusion in male-dominated sports. I use the adjective "nominal" because in most cases there were never any formal rules barring girls and women from joining/trying out for men's teams, or entering individual competitions with men. The National Football League (NFL) was the only US major league sports association that formally excluded women, but it dropped that exclusion in 2012. Where demand is high enough, sex parity in team-based professional sports has taken the form of "sister" leagues such as the WNBA, the LPGA, and the National Women's Soccer League.

These sister leagues have different rules and different conditions. For example, the WNBA uses a smaller basketball than is used in the NBA. The LPGA uses shorter golf courses than those that are used in the PGA. Because nondiscrimination laws must equally apply to male exclusion from nominal women's teams, men are legally permitted to try out for the WNBA and the LPGA, but no man has attempted to do so. The seeming absurdity of this scenario plays out in the B-list Hollywood movie *Juwanna Mann*, in which a professional male basketball player impersonates a woman and tries out for a professional women's basketball team after having been barred from playing in the men's league. Under the alias of Juwanna Mann, Jamal Jeffries makes the women's team and leads them to the national championship. The moral of the story: along the way, he develops empathy and respect for his female teammates and their version of the sport.

While many people, including many feminists, view the creation of girl and women's teams as a positive development, I question the progressiveness of this accommodation. Political scientist Eileen Mc-Donagh and journalist Laura Pappano question this development, too. In their book *Playing with the Boys*, they argue that sex segregation in sports perpetuates gender stereotypes of female inferiority. I ground my position in a consequentialist understanding of feminism that rejects the libertarian view that it's enough merely to open the doors of histori-cally male sports associations, without examining the terms of inclusion. Questioning these terms means examining the social customs that are likely to continue by nominal and extralegal means after assimilation and accommodation have occurred.

The major problem with formal equal opportunity is that it ignores the present-day remnants of historical sexism. McDonagh and Pappano discuss the scientific evidence that women, on average, perform bet-ter in endurance sports than men.[33] Why then has the sex-based ac-commodation in many sports been to shorten the races and duration of other competitive sports? For example, why do men play longer tennis matches than women in major professional tennis tournaments such as the US and Australian Opens?

As in the case of sex-segregated restrooms, some liberal feminists have made the mistake of acquiescing to the sexist premise that the orig-inal male model was in fact "male," and that women needed something different. Did girls need softball instead of baseball? Do they need or want hockey and lacrosse leagues that bar checking? Do female golfers need a shorter course than their male counterparts? Why did we accept the existing standards of male sports as the right standards?

Gendered Spectacle

Equal opportunity is not the only goal we seek in sports. As spectators, we don't want to see just the "best athlete." Many of us are also drawn to the "race-gendered spectacle" of sport, by which I mean the performance of race-specific kinds of masculinity and femininity.

Political theorist Michael Sandel doesn't discuss gender or race, but his analysis of the consumer demand for athletic spectacle is helpful. In Sandel's view, we demand both excellence and striving in the spectacle of sport. On one hand, "excellence consists at least partly in the display of natural talents and gifts that are no doing of the athlete who possesses them." For Sandel, this feature of sport is "an uncomfortable fact for democratic societies" because many of us want to believe that a major component of athletic success is in the striving or effort of individual athletes, and not only in the genetic capacity they inherited from their biological parents.

It's ironic that libertarian philosophers, armchair and academic alike, so often invoke sports as emblematic of meritocracy, when in fact the titans of sports benefit not just from genetic gifts, but also from a host of other advantages that they cannot take personal credit for, such as the luck of having supportive parents with the financial means to pay for expensive training camps and top-flight coaching. To compensate for this "embarrassment," Sandel speculates that "we inflate the moral significance of striving, and depreciate giftedness." He finds strong evidence of this distortion in the coverage of the Olympics by mainstream media, "which focuses less on the feats the athletes perform than on the heart-rending stories of the hardships they have overcome and the struggles they have waged to triumph over an injury or a difficult upbringing or political turmoil in their native land."[34]

Sandel's argument is compelling, but he overlooks the impact of intersectional race-gender norms for how the tension between excellence and striving manifests in particular sports, and at different levels of competition. In the NBA and NFL, what is being marketed is no doubt excellence, but it is in the distinct form of mostly young black men, who are presumed to have heartrending stories of striving to overcome poverty, even though many do not. If a certain kind of black hypermasculinity via sport is the spectacle, then perhaps we should be honest and transparent about what we are demanding in the marketplace of American sport.[35]

Consumer marketing lays bare our race-sex desires vis-à-vis professional athletes. In her 2015 essay "The Meaning of Serena Williams: On Tennis and Black Excellence," Claudia Rankine notes that Maria Sharapova's white feminine appearance has made her more marketable than Serena Williams, despite the fact that Williams is clearly the better tennis player—winning eighteen of their twenty head-to-head matches. Rankine observes,

> There is another, perhaps more important, discussion to be had about what it means to be chosen by global corporations. It has to do with who is worthy, who is desirable, who is associated with the good life. As long as the white imagination markets itself by equating whiteness and blondness with aspirational living, stereotypes will remain fixed in place. Even though Serena is the best, even though she wins more Slams than anyone else, she is only superficially allowed to embody that in our culture, at least the marketable one.[36]

Rankine makes a powerful point here about how professional tennis is marketed. Her argument is compelling and interesting to think about in relation to Renée Richards's biography. What if Richards had been a transgender woman of color from a poor background rather than the person who had been a white male tennis star who attended Yale?

The sex classification of male is not a reliable proxy for masculinity given that female-identified persons can and do embody masculinity, and male-identified people embody and express femininity. Dallas Mavericks owner Mark Cuban made headlines in 2013 when he invited the star women's college basketball player Brittney Griner to try out in the second round of the NBA draft. Many attributed this rare invitation to Griner's masculine physiological features. At a lean, muscular, six feet eight inches tall, Griner defies the statistical stereotype that women are smaller and weaker than men. She also publicly self-identifies as a lesbian, and thus challenges hegemonic feminine norms. Griner declined Cuban's offer, and went on to play in the WNBA for the Phoenix Mercury.

There have been individual women who have attempted to break into male-dominated major league sports. In 2013 Lauren Silberman, who had played women's club soccer at the University of Wisconsin–Madison, became the first woman to try out for the NFL as a kicker. She was unsuccessful and did not try again.[37] Lusia Harris had been selected in the 1978 NBA draft, but declined to join the New Orleans Jazz due to pregnancy.[38] Female goaltender Manon Rhéaume played in a National Hockey League (NHL) exhibition game.[39] Shannon Szabados, also a goaltender, plays professional men's hockey in the Southern Professional Men's Hockey League.[40] No woman has ever played in a regular season NHL game. No woman has ever played in Major League Baseball. Annika Sörenstam became the first woman to play in a PGA tournament, but she did not make the cut. Some sports journalists attributed Sörenstam's failure to the fact that she had spent her entire career playing on the shorter LPGA courses. This raises the stakes in the question about whether female athletes need modified rules, or whether such modifications may actually stunt their development.

A different interpretation of sex-segregated sports is that females do not measure up to males when it comes to professional sports, or when they do, in the case of Griner, they prefer to play in nominal female leagues. But there are so many other layers of explanation to peel back concerning the structures of these organizations, and the institution of American professional sports more generally. There has never been a concerted effort to recruit significant numbers of women to try out for the NHL, NFL, PGA, or NBA. What if Cuban had invited not just Griner, but also several other top professional and NCAA Division I female basketball players to try out for his NBA team? And what if other owners had done likewise at the same time? This might move us beyond the current heroic narrative of one brave individual woman beating the odds, which is a gendered spectacle in itself.

Indeed, some argued against Griner accepting Cuban's offer on the grounds that "it would make a sideshow out of a player who has been considered revolutionary for women's basketball standards."[41] But the sideshow could be avoided if equal opportunity were structured differently. A step in this direction is to contemplate the relationship between sex identity and the administration of sports at various levels. What if we, as spectators, started demanding different kinds of sports stories?

Student Athleticism

Some school sports programs serve as the proving grounds for the launching of professional sports careers. But the vast majority of student-athletes do not follow such a path, a point that the NCAA stresses on its website and in its television commercials. What does the policy goal of promoting student athleticism mean, and how *does* sex classification relate to that goal? Title IX is the most well-known and influential sex-discrimination law governing school-related athletics. Part of the 1972 Education Amendments to the 1964 federal Civil Rights Act, Title IX states that "no person in the United States shall, on the basis of sex, be excluded from participation in, be denied the benefits of, or be subjected to discrimination under any education program or activity receiving Federal financial assistance."[42]

The wording of Title IX has not been amended to include gender identity or gender expression. However, on May 13, 2016, the federal Departments of Justice and Education issued a set of guidelines for how schools should apply Title IX to transgender students in school-sponsored athletics. The wording of the guidelines is worth quoting at length:

Title IX regulations permit a school to operate or sponsor sex-segregated athletics teams when selection for such teams is based upon competitive skill or when the activity involved is a contact sport. A school may not, however, adopt or adhere to requirements that rely on *overly broad generalizations or stereotypes about the differences between transgender students and other students of the same sex (i.e., the same gender identity) or others' discomfort with transgender students.* Title IX does not prohibit age-appropriate, tailored requirements based on sound, current, and research-based medical knowledge about the impact of the students' participation on the competitive fairness or physical safety of the sport. (emphasis added)[43]

With these guidelines, the Obama administration built on its 2009 support for protecting the rights of transgender students under Title IX.

Recall my discussion in chapter 2 of the letter signed by the DOJ and DOE in support of the transgender male student in Arcadia, California, who sued for his right to use the boys' restroom and sleep in the boys' cabin on a school camping trip. Both the 2009 and 2013 letters are important steps forward in the legal support of transgender students. But in both cases the federal government misdiagnosed the scope and source of this sexism. Specifically, it failed to treat sex segregation as sexist. What will schools do in situations where a student either cannot or will not assimilate into a binary sex category, and wants to participate in a school-sponsored athletic program?

The second letter referencing school-sponsored sports can be read as vaguely acknowledging the conceptual distinction between sex classification and the physiological characteristics we associate with binary sex. The letter cautions schools against relying "on overly broad generalizations or stereotypes about the differences between transgender students and other students of the same sex (i.e., the same gender identity) or others' discomfort with transgender students." The relevant "differences" go unspecified but likely pertain to height, weight, and musculature. The letter warns against stereotyping the athletic capacity of transgender students, and also against stereotyping the athletic capacity of "students of the same sex."

It would have been even more helpful if the letter had explicitly connected these dots and questioned the need for sex segregation in school-sponsored sports. Doing so would require an amendment to Title IX, a move that the administration clearly did not want to initiate. In my own questioning of sex segregation, I do not mean to suggest that there is never a need or justification for sex segregation in sports. There may or may not be such a need. It depends on factors such as age, level of play, and specific policy goals. At a minimum, I would like to see individual schools clearly and publicly explain whether and how sex classification is related to their organizational aims.

Recreation

The recreational athlete is (thankfully) far removed from elite amateur and professional sports. Nonetheless, how we administrate sex in this category of sport is important because we recreational athletes outnumber elite athletes by a humungous margin. Physical differences in size and strength are less pronounced between boys and girls prior to puberty, and many parents agree that the main goals for their young children's participation in athletics are exercise and fun. Middle and old age may bring binary sex differences in strength and stamina closer together once again. Many of us who are over thirty-five (or forty-five) no longer wish to participate in cutthroat competitive sports. The star athletic career either never happened or did, and our bodies have paid the price. In the intervening "prime" years, when statistical physiological sex-based differences are much more pronounced, and the competitive stakes are high, a different set of organizational rules might apply.

These peculiarities have made recreational sports an important venue for developing policies regarding transgender inclusion. Adult recreational associations that advertise themselves as queer or LGBT have been on the front lines of this administration because of the inclusion of the T in the LGBT moniker. As a legal matter, a softball league may advertise itself as "lesbian" or "LGBT," but it cannot discriminate against individuals who do not self-identify in these ways. A "women's" soccer league may do a number of things to discourage men from joining their league, but it cannot legally bar a man from joining its ranks. This can pose a challenge to women-only spaces, as we saw in the previous discussion of women's colleges.[44] Maria Pepe's push for inclusion unintentionally paved this legal avenue of transgender inclusion. Recall that the ruling in her case against Little League established that a sports organization effectively becomes a public accommodation when it uses a public park or other sports facility that is open to the public, such as a community ice skating rink or soccer field.

In practice, the main concern regarding transgender inclusion inevitably circles back to competitive dominance. The image of Caster Semenya's "breathtakingly butch" appearance—her flat chest, square jaw, and ripped torso—is the image that many people have in mind when they are asked to include transgender individuals in their sports organizations. But there is considerable physiological variation among transgender women and men. Some transgender women are tall, and some are short. Some play aggressively and are skilled in a given sport, and some don't and aren't. The same goes for transgender men.

When I played in an adult women's ice hockey league in the Midwest in my late twenties and early thirties before changing my sex to male, there was a lot of locker room chatter about a transgender woman who played on one of the teams in our league. Many of my teammates commented on her height and size. Yet, her stature did not translate into good hockey skills. Moreover, although most of us hovered around the average height for US cisgender women, there were several tall women in the league. The DOJ and DOE warned against this kind of intrasexual stereotyping. Our league did not have an official policy regarding transgender inclusion at the time. I don't know if it has since adopted one. It would have been very helpful to explicitly debunk this false stereotype in our bylaws. This would have helped to keep our locker room chatter focused on the matter at issue: is she a good hockey player?

Policy Redesign

The distinction between "sex" and "sex-related" characteristics can help sports administrators redesign policies that are closely tied to their legitimate policy goals.

It is in the best interests of various sports administrative bodies to clearly identify and articulate their objectives and how specific sex-related features matter or do not matter for achieving those goals. Is the main goal to provide a venue for recreational fun, to promote "student athleticism," or to foster elite competition? How does age factor into such goals? What role does commercial revenue play? In discussing and making these decisions, the organization also has an opportunity to think prospectively about people who *might* participate in the organization if its sex-related policies were written and publicized with diverse sex identities in mind.

If an adult recreational sports league wants to be proactive, it could add a statement to its registration forms that conveys its commitment to including people with diverse sex identities. I play tennis with an LGBT adult recreational tennis association. Two years ago, a board member asked me how the club could be more transgender-inclusive in its advertisement and registration materials. I recommended that the club add the following sentences to its mission statement, which appears on its website: "We emphasize recreation and friendly competition, and welcome tennis players of all levels—from beginner to advanced. We also welcome members of all gender identities and expressions, including transgender and gender variant individuals. Our goal is to create an LGBT supportive community space for tennis, friendship and camaraderie." I would describe this as a "proactive" moderate reform. The club is taking steps to explicitly welcome transgender and gender-nonconforming recreational athletes, rather than being "reactive," which would mean waiting until someone made a complaint and dealing with any complaints on a case-by-case, ad hoc basis.

If the club wanted to be "innovative" in its policy reform, I suggested that it both add the above sex-identity inclusive statement and change the sex-identity "choice architecture" of its registration forms. A step in this direction could be to eliminate the M for male or F for female drop-down menu on its online registration form. The intention behind such elimination would be to nudge registrants in the direction of the club's mission: that sex classification is not immediately linked to the club's goals of creating an "LGTB supportive community space for tennis, friendship and camaraderie." At the same time, the club's light focus on competition (we play structured matches and report scores) could be addressed by stressing the importance of specifying one's skill level (A, B, C, D). In doing so, it could give women the option of playing down one level. In fact, this is the official policy of the GLTA (Gay and Lesbian Tennis Association). The GLTA should also add "transgender" to its title; its T stands for tennis.

If an elite competitive athletic association wants to adopt a "proactive" policy reform, it might consider adding an official statement to its bylaws and to all of its bureaucratic forms that conveys a commitment to inclusion. If such an organization wants to adopt an "innovative" policy reform, it could change the structure of competition. So, for example, if the IOC wants to keep its current policy of using functional testosterone levels as the most important and deciding sex-related feature in the Olympic Games, then it should follow that policy to its logical conclusion: men with low levels of testosterone should be permitted to compete in women's events, if they so choose. To reflect the new policy, the IOC could replace the terms "men" and "women" with terms that more precisely convey the notion of "sex-related" features.

When the competitive stakes are high, policy makers should consider using physiological features such as height, weight, and, in the case of elite athletes over the age of eighteen, androgen levels as sorting measures. In professional sports the focus should be on questioning our con-sumer demand for race-gendered athletic spectacles. Should we make different demands in the lucrative business of sports?

When the competitive stakes are low or nonexistent and the focus is on recreation and fun, then sports organizations should think about and clearly articulate if and how sex identity relates to those goals. Sex-based social affinity might be relevant to an adult recreational tennis associa-tion. But it is not enough to make this claim; the organization should also be transparent about the definition of sex identity it is invoking, and make clear how it intends to comply with sex discrimination laws.

Conclusion

Sex segregation directly harms many intersex and transgender athletes and would-be athletes. But, these policies also harm many cisgender people who do not see a place for themselves in certain sports because they sense and are told by parents, peers, teachers, and coaches that they do not measure up to the normative masculinities and feminini-ties that we attach to those sports. As we have seen in previous chapters, the material evidence of binary sex is not always visible, measurable, or stable over time.

As I write this final case study, the closing ceremonies of the 2016 Rio Summer Olympic Games draw near. It has been a remarkable spectacle of sport. I am in awe of the beautiful bodies of these elite athletes—the diversity of their sport-specific attributes. From the short and muscular gymnasts to the emaciated long-distance runners, the ectomorph vol-leyball stars, the broad-backed swimmers, the heavy-set weightlifters and shot putters. Caster Semenya is back at her sport and won the gold medal in the women's eight-hundred-meter race. Her presence on the track tells us that she passed the functional testosterone test. I smile as I see she's wearing the spandex one-piece jumpsuit that has become the de facto uniform for male sprinters. Her competitors don the two-piece spandex "bikini" that has become the de facto uniform for female runners of all distances. I wonder if this was a choice motivated by a sense of humor or personal comfort, or both. The outfit and her speed set her apart from the other mid-distance elite female sprinters—but not too far apart. For, there are many similarities among them. Semenya's muscles are ripped, but so are theirs.

Conclusion

Silence on the Bus

The sex-classification policies explored in this book are just a small sample of the many other sex-classification policies that orchestrate US public life. My hope is that organizational leaders and activists can draw lessons from my four case studies that can help them to bring about institutional change in their own organizations. As transgender people become more visible in US culture, many liberal and progressive people express general support for transgender civil rights. However, many are unclear or misguided about what practical steps are needed to ensure that transgender and gender-nonconforming people can participate in the public sphere on equal terms with the cisgender majority.[1]

The foregoing analysis corrects some of this misunderstanding by digging down to the root of sex-identity discrimination: the administration of sex. The case studies show why and how sex-classification policies trigger sex-identity discrimination, and why we would all be better served by alternative policies that are more clearly articulated and aligned with legitimate institutional goals. The legally inspired diagnostic test of harm and necessity and livable policy design are generalizable and can be used by anyone interested in making organizations more transgender-inclusive and better for everyone.

The sequencing of the case studies was meant to show how all sex-classification policies are imbricated. Or, perhaps more accurately, they envelop one another. Birth certificates are necessary for obtaining driver's licenses, state identification cards, and passports. These are directly and indirectly referenced in the arguments of those who seek to bar transgender people from public restroom use, and those who seek to preserve women-only admissions for certain private colleges. In the world of sports, where sex-based assumptions and physiology are so explicitly at the center of policy, testosterone levels have become the proxy for determining whether women may compete in women's elite athletic competition.

When we applied the diagnostic test of harm and necessity to government-issued personal identity documents, it was easy to expose the faulty logic. Sex markers were not "rationally" related to the legitimate and important governmental goal of personal identity verification because sex identity is personally changeable and there are better ways for the government and others to verify our personal identities in situations where the risks of identity theft are high. Exposing this faulty logic, nevertheless, does not mean that it will be easy to convince policy makers to remove these sex markers from our birth certificates, driver's licenses, and passports.

This is because removing the sex markers from such documents is tantamount to extracting the first card that topples the house of cards that is sex classification. The vast majority of people will never have the sex markers on these documents inspected by an administrative agent. But for people who appear to be transgender, the risk of such inspection is high, and so are the stakes of such scrutiny. The sex markers are right there on our documents for agents to inspect. Whether they do so or not depends on the particular agent. The mechanism of sex-identity discrimination is precisely this discretion. The moderately liberal legal strategies of assimilation and accommodation are inadequate because they fail to address this problem. Male or female markers should not be made available for administrative agents to draw upon in their misbegotten role of sex-identity verifiers.

Sex-classification policies are material artifacts that were conceived and codified by people, and thus can be rewritten and overwritten by the same people or their successors. As I have shown, more often than not the use of sex on bureaucratic forms or to physically segregate people is habitual rather than the product of strategic thinking about why and how sex is relevant to organizational aims, and why and how the use of sex is discriminatory.

Personal identity documents should keep track of particular persons, regardless of the sex-related physical changes people undergo in their lifetimes. When it comes to public restrooms, we all just need a modicum of privacy and safety to tend to our bodily functions and those of the people in our care. Women's colleges should be renamed "historically women's colleges" and evaluate prospective students' personal commitments to their feminist institutional values, regardless of sex identity. Certain sex-related physical features are sometimes relevant to sports. But this depends on age and the level of play.

When sex classification is relevant, policy makers should clearly explain what definition of sex and/or gender they are asking us to use to check a bureaucratic box, or what definition of these terms they are using in their own third-person evaluations of us. An excellent example of such an explanation is the new patient registration form used by the Fenway Health Center in Boston, which is dedicated to providing health care to the lesbian, gay, bisexual, and transgender community. The registration form asks patients to check a female or male box. But it follows up that request with a clear explanation of *why* it is asking for this information, and what definition of "legal sex" patients should use in checking a box. The health clinic needs to collect a certain kind of sex-identity information because many insurance companies require that information, along with the patient's "legal name," to process the patient's claims. By contrast, Fenway "recognizes a number of genders/ sexes." It defers to the patient's first-person sense of their sex identity: "If your preferred name and pronouns are different from these, please let us know." Collecting this information is important so that the health clinic can communicate clearly and respectfully with its patients about their health care.

This is a strong example of a transgender-inclusive intake form. It follows the principles of feminist "choice architecture." And it follows universal design because it uses transgender and gender-nonconforming

FENWAY ⊞ HEALTH Client Registration	The information in your medical record is confidential and is protected under Massachusetts General Laws Ch. 111, Sec 70. Your written consent will be required for release of information except in the case of a court order.	Medical Record # *(For office use only)*
Legal Name* Last	First	Middle Initial	Name used:

Legal Sex (please check one)* ☐ Female ☐ Male	Pronouns:
While Fenway recognizes a number of genders / sexes, many insurance companies and legal entities unfortunately do not. Please be aware that the name and sex you have listed on your insurance must be used on documents pertaining to insurance, billing and correspondence. If your preferred name and pronouns are different from these, please let us know.	

Fenway Health Center patient registration form.

experience to bring about a policy change that makes everyone better off. Cisgender gender-conforming patients also benefit from the explanation of why the clinic is asking them to check a sex-identity box, and how they will use that information. We should all know these things.

Pragmatism and organizational efficiency are helpful motivating tools for bringing about institutional change. At the same time, we must not forget the experiences of those who suffer when we fail to act on their behalf. As Judith Butler writes, "It is not a question of blinding oneself to how a person appears, but a question instead of how the way in which a person appears blinds one to the worth and capability of the person. The radical consequence of law, conceived as social practice, is to make us pause, and pause again, as we enter into the risky process of knowing and judging one another."[2]

I close with a personal note that does not put me in my best light, but also stands as a testament to the strength of social forces allied against those of us who are perceived to be transgender. Five years ago, after a long day of work, I took the C bus, which runs from Temple University down Broad Street, the city's north-south spine, to Center City, where I used to live. A few streets from my stop, Charlene boarded. The bus driver did not call her back to ask loud questions about her sex identity, and whether he thought it matched the sex sticker on her monthly transit pass. Today seemed to be a good day, at least that's how things looked from where I sat. She took a seat next to someone near the front of the cabin, a few rows of blue-fabric seating in front of where I slumped from fatigue, enjoying some pop music with speakers in my ears, my personal sound system. But not even Rihanna could compete with the diesel bus as it heaved through its angry gear cycle, creating a muffled background for the automated street announcements of upcoming streets we had already passed. We were mostly a bunch of tired commuters at that time of day rumbling through the city.

But when Charlene joined us, most people stared at her, glared really, and I watched confusion and disdain colonize faces that had just seconds before been blank, perhaps even civil. Charlene's bearing in response was regal and humble, the posture of a veteran holding familiar ground in a prolonged war of wills, bracing for the predictable snickers, and possibly worse, because she had known that, too. She wore a long African-print dress to match dreadlocks neatly held in place with a scarf: the sartorial antithesis of the attention-hungry stereotyped "drag queen," just a middle-aged conservatively attired black woman on her way home from work, weary like the rest of us. My shame in telling this story is that I should have risen and walked over to tap Charlene gently on the shoulder to say hello, as we had worked together on a few transgender activist projects in the city, and were on friendly terms. She always had a ready hug. "I don't shake hands," her cheerful adherence to one simple feminine norm. I could say I was too tired, or that the bus was too crowded. But the more truthful explanation is that I worried that I too might land in the crosshairs of the bus riders' aggressive stares. Ah-ha! Look, he's one of them, too!

ACKNOWLEDGMENTS

Writing a book is, in many ways, a lonely sojourn. But others walk with you. I'm grateful to the many colleagues, students, friends, and loved ones who walked with me, and helped me find ways around and over various hurdles.

To my wife, Samantha Korn, thank you for many conversations about this project—its content, yes, but more importantly for being there in the not so pretty times of frustration and angst. Thanks to Reuel Rogers, for our decades-long friendship and countless conversations about politics, race, and masculinities. Thanks to Christy Schneider, my dear friend and Philly expert, for all of our chinwags about gender and SEPTA.

In the early going, my colleagues and friends Sara Rushing, Lori Marso, Cristina Beltran, Samantha Majic, Susan Burgess, and Rita Dhamoon were kind and generous enough to take the time to read through my scattered thoughts and help me make sense of them. I owe a shout-out to the Feminist Political Theory Workshop that gathers every year in a big circle the day before the Western Political Science Association (WPSA) conference. For years, we've read and discussed one another's work and offered support. Thanks for being my community. Thanks also to Cathy Hannabach for her incredibly helpful research assistance.

This book grew out of my article "Sex-Classification Policies as Transgender Discrimination: An Intersectional Critique," published in 2014 in *Perspectives on Politics*. I'm grateful to the journal's editor, Jeffrey Isaacs, and to the anonymous reviewers, all of whom gave me thoughtful and immensely useful critical feedback. I presented an earlier version of that article at the WPSA meetings in 2010, and was honored to win the Betty Nesvold Award for the Best Paper on Women and Politics. Thank you, Tamara Metz, for inviting me to give a talk based on that paper at Reed

College and for your helpful words of advice. Thanks, Liz Markovits, for welcoming me into your Feminist Political Theory seminar via Skype. The technology failed us, but we made it work, nevertheless. I learned so much from you and your razor-sharp Mount Holyoke students. I also joined Amrita Basu's Amherst seminar via Skype. Not only did your students fix our technology problems, but they also had terrific insights and queries that have made this book better than it might have been.

Back at my home base in Philadelphia, I'm grateful to my Temple University colleagues and our students who gave up their Friday after- noon to hear me talk about sex and bathrooms. Some of the research for this book was supported by a Summer Research Award from Temple University. Thanks to Joel Schlosser and Paulina Ochoa Espejo for invit- ing me to present an earlier draft of this book's introduction at the TriCo Political Theory Colloquium at Haverford College. It was a lively and ed- ifying conversation with good colleagues. I'm grateful to Charlotte Pat- terson for inviting me to give the Bernard Mayes LGBTQ Lecture at the Women and Gender Studies Department at the University of Virginia in 2016. There, I presented an earlier draft of chapter 1. During my visit, I also presented a paper based on the book's main argument at UVA's Political Theory Workshop. I'm thankful to everyone who attended and offered me critical feedback. A special thanks to Brittany Leach who served as the graduate student discussant for my presentation, and to Corrine Field, Andre Calvacante, Denise Walsh, and Lawrie Balfour for our more in-depth conversations about the book's argument and scope. Thank you, Rose Corrigan, for inviting me to present the work at Drexel University's Law and Society Reading Group, and to the Drexel Law fac- ulty who gave me helpful feedback. And thank you, Jennifer Parks, for inviting me to deliver the John Grant Lecture in Health Care Ethics at Loyola University, where I discussed "Sex-Classification in Health Care Administration: Transgender and Genderqueer Perspectives."

A big thank-you to my editor, Ilene Kalish, for believing in me and for much-needed laughs along the way, and to Caelyn Cobb for all of her editorial assistance.

I have the Philly trans activist community to thank, too. When I transitioned from female to male nine years ago, I was referred to the support/advocacy group T-MAN (Trans-Masculine Advocacy Network). We met every Monday night to talk about anything and everything. Our slogan, "What kind of man are you?," stays with me as I know it does for all of you. Thank you for handshakes and hugs, and most of all for being just a text or phone call away. It was through my work with T-MAN that I was fortunate enough to meet Charlene Arcila. She was an intrepid advocate for transgender civil rights and people living and struggling with HIV/AIDS in Philly and beyond. In 2016 we lost Charlene, but her life's work and kind soul remain here in the "city of brotherly love, and sisterly affection."

APPENDIX

The Gender Audit: A How-to Guide for Organizations

I work with individuals and organizations to help them design sex-classification policies that are tailored to their organizational needs and aspirations. Below, I share some of the workshop materials I use. I hope they might be helpful to readers who are looking for pragmatic ways to make their organizations more inclusive of people with diverse sex identities. I also share the results of a gender audit I conducted for a corporate bank, so that readers can get a visual sense of the audit.

THE WORKSHOP

Description
The first ninety-minute workshop builds critical awareness about the different identities beneath the umbrella term "transgender," and the forms of direct and indirect discrimination that trans people face in the United States. Sometimes sex classification is relevant to a particular organizational or individual goal, and sometimes it isn't. Through critical self-reflective and small-group brainstorming exercises, we perform audits of how and why sex is directly and indirectly invoked in the policies of the organizations where we work, and in our own individual practices. In the second ninety-minute workshop, participants are introduced to the principle of inclusive policy design, and practice using it to develop a trans-inclusive policy or practice that benefits everyone affected by the policy.

Informational Handout

This handout provides a general overview and definition of important terms related to making your professional practices and organizational policies inclusive of transgender identities.

1. What Is Transgender?

Each one of us was assigned a sex classification at birth. This is the male or female sex marker that appears on our original birth certificate. The term "transgender" describes the experience of changing one's birth sex classification. Currently (as of November 2016), every state except for Tennessee makes it possible for a person to change her or his birth certificate sex marker from female to male or male to female. The requirements for doing so vary somewhat, but generally require some form of medical intervention (surgery/hormones/letter from a medical practitioner).

The term "legal sex" often refers to our birth sex classification. However, other official "legal" forms of identity documents include driver's licenses, state identification cards, and passports. All states allow for the sex markers on these identity documents to be changed. Some require medical intervention, and some do not. An important thing to note is that some trans people have changed all of these official sex markers, some have changed one or two of them, and some have not changed any of these documents.

SEX: How a person identifies, or is identified, in relation to the categories of male or female, or both.

GENDER: How a person expresses, or is perceived as expressing, the concepts of masculinity and femininity (e.g., clothing, haircut, mannerisms, comportment).

CISGENDER: A person who does not identify as transgender.

GENDER CONFORMING: A person (trans or cisgender) whose appearance and behavior conforms to prevailing expectations (e.g., a masculine boy or a feminine woman).

GENDER NONCONFORMING: A person (trans or cisgender) whose appearance and/or behavior challenges prevailing expectations (e.g., a feminine boy or a masculine woman).

GENDER IDENTITY: This term can be confusing. In my work, I prefer to use the term "sex identity." Gender identity nondiscrimination laws vary in their wording, but generally they are enhanced, more detailed sex discrimination laws. For example, Philadelphia's Fair Practices Ordinance defines gender identity as "self-perception, or perception by others, as male or female," which includes "an individual's appearance, behavior, or physical characteristics, that may be in accord with, or opposed to one's physical anatomy, chromosomal sex, or sex assigned at birth; and shall include, but not be limited to, individuals who are undergoing or have completed sex reassignment." The discrimination being pinpointed here, in my view, is more accurately described as *sex-identity* discrimination because it involves judgments about whether a person belongs to the sex categories of male or female. By contrast, traditional sexism is based on judgments about what we can and cannot do *because* we are male or female. These "scripts for identity" are what we commonly refer to as *gender* stereotypes.

2. What Is Transgender Discrimination?

SEX DISCRIMINATION: Invidious treatment "because of sex"; stereotypes about what people can and cannot or should and should not do because they are female or male.

GENDER IDENTITY DISCRIMINATION: Judgments about whether or not a person is female or male.

INTERACTIVE WORKSHOP MATERIALS

Worksheet 1: How to Conduct a Gender Audit
How is sex classification invoked in your workplace? These can be formal or informal policies and practices. List as many as you can.
Example 1: Sex classification question on clinical intake form (formal)
Example 2: The use of gendered pronouns (he, she, him, her) (informal)

3. _____

4. _____

5. _____

6. _____

7. _____

8. _____

9. _____

10. _____

Worksheet 2: Evaluating the Necessity of Sex-Classification Policies and Practices
Together in small groups, select three policies/practices from Worksheet 1 and list them in the boxes below. For each, discuss and determine the main goal. Is sex classification necessary for achieving the policy/practice goal? If the answer is no, then check "eliminate." If the answer is yes, check "keep but maybe redesign."

Policy/Practice	Goal	Eliminate	Keep but Maybe Redesign
Example: sex-segregated restrooms	*Privacy and safety for staff and clients*		X

Worksheet 3: Trans-Inclusive Design Challenge
Together in small groups, select one policy/practice from Worksheet 2 that you would keep but maybe redesign. Note the policy/practice and its goal below. Then, discuss how you could redesign the policy/practice so that it is inclusive of the most expansive universe of sex identities. Then, below the chart note the benefits to people with other identities.

Policy/Practice	Goal	Redesigned Policy/Practice
Example: sex-segregated restrooms	*Privacy and safety for staff and clients*	*New construction: build all-gender restrooms*

Benefits to people with other identities:

_____

_____

_____

_____

_____

What follows are the results of a gender audit I prepared for a corporate bank. I arranged them by level of difficulty. Within each policy column I also provide two options for an organization to consider: proactive and innovative.

Sample Policy Recommendations: Level 1

	Employee Handbook	Employee Identification Cards	Surveys	Employee Records
Goals	Clear communication of employee obligations	Verification of employees' personal (not gender) identity to ensure firm security	Survey specific	Personal identity verification; employee privacy
Proactive	Replace M/F pronouns with "the employee"; rewrite necessary/relevant gender references for clarity + context (e.g., dress code)	Make photo and name updating streamlined	Remove all irrelevant gender pronouns and questions; add contextual language to explain all relevant/ necessary gender questions	Eliminate sex-identity markers where feasible
Innovative	Add statement reiterating the firm's strong commitment to affirming the self-reported gender identity of all employees	Use biometric technologies instead of photos to verify personal identities	Add statement reiterating the firm's strong commitment to affirming the self-reported gender identity of all employees	Add contextual language to all necessary/ relevant gender markers
Points of contact	Human Resources	Human Resources + outside vendor	Managers, network leaders; Human Resources	Human Resources

Sample Policy Recommendations: Level 2

	Dental Insurance	Health Insurance	Recruitment
Goals	Effective coverage; personal identity verification	Effective coverage; personal identity verification	Finding, hiring, and retaining best talent
Proactive	Add contextual language to all gender questions	Verify coverage of all gender-confirming health care (surgeries, hormone therapy); evaluate definition of "cosmetic" procedures	Clearly convey the firm's commitment to trans awareness + gender identity diversity; make the net-work's video available and prominent in all recruitment efforts
Innovative	Remove gender mark-ers from intake forms	Remove gender mark-ers from procedures such as OB-GYN care and prostate exams	Convey to recruiters the importance of finding diverse slates of candidates that are trans inclusive
Points of contact	Human Resources + in-surance carrier + net-work/out-of-network dental practices	Human Resources + insurance carrier + network/out-of-network physicians	Managers, Human Re-sources + recruiters

Sample Policy Recommendations: Level 3

	Health Clinic	Restrooms	Gym Locker/ Restrooms	Meetings
Goals	Effective com-munication to deliver good health care	Privacy + safety	Privacy + safety	Effective communication
Proactive	Eliminate use of sex markers as proxies for genitals and reproductive organs; add con-textual language to all gender questions (e.g., intake forms)	Notify employees that they have the right to use the restroom that matches their gender self-definition	Notify employees that they have the right to use the restroom/ locker room that matches their gender self-definition	Managers + proj-ect leads could ask individuals to confirm their gender identity via private com-munication; a standard form could be created
Innovative	Ask gender pro-noun preference on intake form	Redesign gender-neutral/"all gender" facilities that ensure individual privacy and safety (e.g., floor-to-ceiling stall partitions + common hand-washing and mirror area)	Redesign gender-neutral/"all gender" facilities that ensure individual privacy and safety	Introduce gender pronoun prefer-ence check-ins when new people join the team/ meeting
Points of contact	Outside vendor?	Facilities + architect	Outside vendor?; facilities + architect	Managers/proj-ect leads

Master Document

	Handbook	Identification Cards	Health Center	Record Keeping	Restrooms	Health Insurance	Dental Insurance	Recruitment	Meetings	Surveys	Gym Locker/Restroom
Policy goals	Clear communication of employee obligations	Personal identity verification of employees to ensure firm security	Effective communication to deliver good health care	Personal identity verification; privacy	Privacy + safety	Effective coverage; personal identity verification	Effective coverage; personal identity verification	Finding, hiring, and retaining best talent	Effective communication	Collecting and crunching specific data	Privacy + safety
Proactive reform	Replace M/F pronouns with "the employee"; rewrite necessary gender references for clarity + context	Keep photo and name updated	Eliminate use of sex markers as proxies for genitals and reproductive organs; add contextual language to all sex-identity questions (e.g., intake forms)	Add contextual language to all sex-identity questions	Add language regarding gender identity to handbook	Verify coverage of all gender-confirming health care	Add contextual language to all sex-identity questions	Clearly convey the firm's commitment to gender identity diversity; make the network's video available and prominent	Managers + project leads could ask individuals to confirm their GI via private communication; a standard form could be created	Remove all irrelevant sex-identity questions; add contextual language to all relevant/necessary sex-identity questions	Private shower and change stalls
Radical reform	Add statement reiterating the firm's strong commitment to affirming the self-reported gender identity of all	Use biometric technologies instead of photos	Ask gender pronoun preference on intake form	Eliminate sex-identity markers where feasible	Convert to gender-neutral/"all gender" facilities; floor-to-ceiling stall partitions + common hand-washing and mirror area	Remove sex markers from procedures such as OB-GYN care and prostate exams	Remove sex markers from intake forms	Convey to headhunters the importance of finding diverse slates of candidates	Gender pronoun preference check-ins become routinized	Replace M/F pronouns with "the employee"; rewrite necessary gender references for clarity + context	Convert to gender-neutral/"all gender" facilities
Stakeholders	HR	Facilities; outside vendor	Outside vendor?	HR	Facilities	HR + physicians	HR + dental practices	Managers, especially diversity + HR + headhunters	Managers/project leads	Managers + network leaders	Outside vendor?

NOTES

INTRODUCTION

1 Charlene passed away in 2015. The city and the transgender activist community lost a pioneer. She founded the Philadelphia Trans-Health Conference, the largest transgender conference in the nation. She was an ordained minister, and worked for many years in Philadelphia to make the city a better place for us all.

2 *Transpass.*

3 Philadelphia Commission on Human Relations, "Public Accommodations Discrimination."

4 Appiah, "Stereotypes and the Shaping of Identity."

5 Denvir, "SEPTA's Gender Discrimination."

6 Nussbaum, "City to Probe Transit Rider's Gender ID Complaint."

7 Riders Against Gender Exclusion, "R.A.G.E.: About Us."

8 *Transpass.*

9 Ibid.

10 Ibid.

11 Ibid.

12 Southeastern Pennsylvania Transportation Authority, "Board Approves Fare Increases."

13 As of this writing, the legal challenge is still pending because SEPTA contends that it is not subject to Philadelphia's gender identity antidiscrimination law because it operates public vehicles outside of the city. Neither the state of Pennsylvania nor the federal government bans gender identity discrimination in public accommodations. The Pennsylvania Supreme Court has agreed to hear the case to settle the dispute over jurisdiction.

14 Marder, "Transgender Riders Seek Justice from SEPTA."

15 Serano, *Whipping Girl,* 41.

16 Grant et al., "Injustice at Every Turn."

17 Ibid.

18 Brydum, "N.J. Trans Woman Murdered"; Haywood, "Update."

19 Brownstone, "New Report Highlights Police Hostility."

20 Threadcraft, "Black Female Body."

21 Serano, *Whipping Girl,* 42.

22 Spade, "Keynote Address," 369.

23 Davis, *Contesting Intersex.*

24 For a discussion of variations in first-person sex identities, see Bornstein, *Gender Outlaw*; Sycamore, *That's Revolting!*; Diamond, *From the Inside Out.*

CHAPTER 1. THE SEX MARKERS WE CARRY

1 Leff, "Transgender ID Cards."
2 Pieklo, "Illinois Consent Decree Important Step."
3 Huppke, "Transgender People Sue Illinois to Change Birth Certificates."
4 *Transpass.*
5 Currah and Spade, "State We're In," 3.
6 General Assembly of North Carolina, "Session Law 2016–3 House Bill 2."
7 See, for example, first-wave feminist texts such as Wollstonecraft, *Vindication of the Rights of Woman*; Stanton, *Solitude of Self*; Stanton, *Woman's Bible*. Also see second-wave feminist texts such as Friedan, *Feminine Mystique*; Okin, *Justice, Gender, and the Family.*
8 I borrow the term "the demands of femininity" from Lori Marso, "Feminism's Quest for Common Desires."
9 For example, feminist legal scholar Catharine MacKinnon describes the relationship between men and women as one of sexual dominance. She argues that women, as a class, are oppressed by men, as a class, via sex. Bluntly, "Man fucks woman. Subject verb object." MacKinnon, *Feminism Unmodified.*
10 Fausto-Sterling, *Sexing the Body*; Lacqueur, *Making Sex.*
11 See, for example, Chodorow, *Femininities, Masculinities, Sexualities.*
12 Roberts, *Fatal Intervention*; Roberts, *Killing the Black Body.*
13 Butler, *Undoing Gender*; Butler and Athanasiou, *Dispossession.*
14 Beauchamp and D'Harlingue, "Beyond Additions and Exceptions."
15 See, for examples, Anzalone, *U.S. Supreme Court Cases on Gender and Sexual Equality.*
16 See, for example, *United States v. Virginia.*
17 Sheridan and O'Keefe, "Parentage Goes 'Gender Neutral' on Passport Form."
18 See, for example, Sacramento County Health and Human Services, "Out-of-Hospital Birth Registration."
19 Intersex Society of North America, "How Common Is Intersex?"
20 Karkazis, *Fixing Sex.*
21 Fausto-Sterling, *Sexing the Body.*
22 For personal memoirs recounting the damaging effects of such denial of sex-identity self-authority, see Colapinto, *As Nature Made Him*; Hillman, *Intersex.*
23 Davis, *Contesting Intersex.*
24 Intersex Society of North America, "Our Mission."
25 Karkazis, *Fixing Sex*, 9.
26 Scott, *Seeing Like a State.*
27 The passage of the 1935 Social Security Act ushered in the first of these programs, which included old age financial assistance and unemployment insurance. During

the Second World War, the federal government expanded its welfare programming to the provision of food rations and family allowances, both of which were based upon the number of "live births" in a household. These incentives, coupled with an extensive federal campaign aimed at encouraging physicians and individuals to register live births, yielded a dramatic increase in the number of people with birth certificates.

28 Spade, "Documenting Gender."
29 In the US Constitution, any power not explicitly granted to the federal government falls into the hands of the individual states.
30 Spade, "Documenting Gender."
31 This is due to the size of birth certificates and passports, and also the fact that these two documents are more difficult to replace in the event that they are lost or stolen.
32 National Center for Transgender Equality, "Department of Homeland Security REAL ID Final Regulations"; REAL ID Act (2005).
33 Robertson, *Passport in America.*
34 US Department of State, "How to Apply for a Passport."
35 Hauser, "President's Column," 22.
36 "New York Ousts 'Race' from Forms."
37 *Des Moines Register* Editorial Board, "Editorial."
38 Brase, "Not Just a Birth Certificate."
39 The origin of strict scrutiny can be traced back to footnote 4 of the Supreme Court case *United States v. Carolene Products Co.* There the Court states that "discrete and insular minorities . . . may call for a correspondingly more searching judicial scrutiny."
40 *Craig v. Boren.*
41 Laurie Shrage, for example, argues that the government does not need to know our sex identities, but then calls for a sex marker amendment rather than eradication. Shrage, "Does the Government Need to Know Your Sex?"
42 Link and Raz, *What Becomes You.*
43 California Department of Public Health, "Obtaining a New Birth Certificate after Gender Reassignment."
44 Currah and Moore, "'We Won't Know Who You Are,'" 118.
45 Ibid., 119.
46 Ibid., 124.
47 Avi, "New York State Updates Birth Certificate Policy."
48 Allen, "Quest for Acceptance," 184.
49 Here, I critique Mottet's moderate liberal reformist argument. Mottet, "Modernizing State Vital Statistics Statutes and Policies."
50 Transgender Law Center, "Kansas Woman Sues State."
51 Transgender Law Center, "DMV Again Settles."
52 US Department of State, "New Policy on Gender Change in Passports Announced."

53 Australian Passport Office, "Sex and Gender Diverse Passport Applicants."
54 Beard, "Germany."
55 Halberstam, *Female Masculinity*, 27.
56 Shrage, "Does the Government Need to Know Your Sex?"
57 Some radical feminists make this argument. See, for example, Goldberg, "What Is a Woman?"
58 Erickson-Schroth, *Trans Bodies, Trans Selves*.
59 See Thompson, *Schematic State*.
60 Lyon, *Identifying Citizens*.
61 Finn, *Capturing the Criminal Image*.

CHAPTER 2. BATHROOM BOUNCERS

1 Lee, "Sexual Stereotypes, Civil Rights and a Suit about Both."
2 *Transpass*.
3 General Assembly of North Carolina, "Session Law 2016–3 House Bill 2."
4 Appiah, "Stereotypes and the Shaping of Identity."
5 Lee, "Sexual Stereotypes, Civil Rights and a Suit about Both."
6 Coyote, "Fear and Loathing in Public Bathrooms."
7 Frosch, "In Colorado, a Legal Dispute over Transgender Rights."
8 Rubin Erdely, "Six-Year-Old Who Wants to Change Gender."
9 Associated Press, "Nicole Maines, Transgender Student."
10 Herman, "Gendered Restrooms and Minority Stress," 65.
11 Individuals without homes are "comprehensively unfree," meaning that they literally have no place to *be*. Waldron, "Homelessness and the Issue of Freedom." See also Feldman, *Citizens without Shelter*.
12 New York City Human Rights Law.
13 New York State Human Rights Law.
14 Many states had sodomy laws on their books, which criminalized "non-procreative" sex acts. These laws were used to target and prosecute gays and lesbians, but their wording applied to everyone. The Supreme Court upheld such laws in the 1986 case *Bowers v. Hardwick*, and overturned that ruling in the 2003 case *Lawrence v. Texas*.
15 Alcoff, *Visible Identities*, 6.
16 Lovehall, "Passing as a Transsexual Black Man."
17 Kogan, "Sex Separation."
18 Greed, "Creating a Nonsexist Restroom."
19 Case, "Why Not Abolish Laws of Urinary Segregation?"
20 Bickford, "Constructing Inequality"; Kohn, *Brave New Neighborhoods*.
21 Frank, "Anti-trans Bathroom Nightmare Has Its Roots in Racial Segregation."
22 Gay, "Seduction of Safety, on Campus and Beyond."
23 "Girl, 7, Raped and Slain."
24 Currah, "New Transgender Panic."

25 Lee, "Woman Wins a Settlement."
26 Geidner, "Federal Officials Protect Transgender Student Against Discrimination."
27 Davidson, "Bill Would Ban Transgender Bathroom Use in Schools."
28 *New York Times* Editorial Board, "Transgender Law Makes North Carolina Pioneer in Bigotry."
29 Butler, *Undoing Gender*.
30 NBC10 and Wire Reports, "Gender-Neutral Restrooms Become the Law."
31 Moran, "Evanston Becomes 7th U.S. City."
32 US Department of Justice, "Guidance on the 2010 ADA Standards."
33 Anna Kirkland argues that the real animus against transgender people is that they are aesthetically shocking. Kirkland, "What's at Stake in Transgender Discrimination as Sex Discrimination?"
34 Arneil, "Disability, Self-Image, and Modern Political Theory."
35 Silber, "McCrory Defends Controversial New Law."
36 Kogan, "Sex Separation."
37 Case, "Why Not Abolish Laws of Urinary Segregation?"
38 Ibid.
39 Malone, "Gender Benders."
40 Hamraie, "Designing Collective Access."
41 Political theorist Joan Tronto makes a compelling argument that care is a fundamental democratic principle. See Tronto, *Caring Democracy*.
42 US Department of Justice, Civil Rights Division, "Advisory, Toilet Rooms and Bathing Rooms."

CHAPTER 3. CHECKING A SEX BOX TO GET INTO COLLEGE

1 "Calliope Wong Discusses Smith College's Exclusion."
2 Adalman, "Prominent Women's Colleges."
3 "Calliope Wong Discusses Smith College's Exclusion."
4 Feldman, "Who Are Women's Colleges For?"
5 Quart, "When Girls Will Be Boys."
6 Padawer, "When Women Become Men at Wellesley."
7 Catharine MacKinnon argues that mainstream feminist arguments miss the fact that male sexual dominance and female sexual subordination define the categories of male and female. See MacKinnon, *Feminism Unmodified*.
8 Goldberg, "What Is a Woman?"
9 "Putting a Face to Calliope Wong."
10 Chen, "Health Effects of Transitioning."
11 Rubin Erdely, "Six-Year-Old Who Wants to Change Gender."
12 Associated Press, "Nicole Maines, Transgender Student."
13 Geidner, "Transgender Breakthrough."
14 See, for example, Snorton, "'A New Hope.'"
15 Ring, "This Year's Michigan Womyn's Music Festival Will Be the Last."

16 US Department of Education, "Title IX and Sex Discrimination."
17 Feldman, "Who Are Women's Colleges For?"
18 Associated Press, "US Women's Colleges Change Admission Policies."
19 Jaschik, "2 Christian Colleges Win Title IX Exemptions."
20 Recently, some Asian Americans have argued that they are being discriminated against in the form of admissions quotas limiting their numbers. Nevertheless, sociologists Jennifer Lee and Min Zhou argue that race-based affirmative action is in the best interests of Asian Americans given that they still suffer from institutional racism. Survey data show that the majority of Asian Americans favor race-based affirmative action. Lee and Zhou, *Asian American Achievement Paradox*.
21 *Regents of the University of California v. Bakke* (1978).
22 Jaschik, "Affirmative Action for Men."
23 *United States v. Virginia*.
24 Ibid.
25 Hennessey, "What's in a Women's College?"
26 Mount Holyoke College, "Admission of Transgender Students."
27 Smith College, "About Smith."
28 Barnard College, "Admissions."
29 The other two are Barber-Scotia College and Bethune-Cookman University.
30 Spelman College, "Spelman College Mission Statement."
31 Bennett College, "Bennett College Mission and Philosophy."
32 Wabash College, "Wabash College Mission Statement."
33 Hampden-Sydney College, "Hampden-Sydney College Mission Statement."
34 Morehouse College, "Morehouse College Mission."
35 King, "Mean Girls of Morehouse."
36 Feldman, "Who Are Women's Colleges For?"
37 Harris, "Barnard College."
38 Callahan, "Trans Women."
39 Padawer, "When Women Become Men at Wellesley."
40 Sara Ahmed cautions that diversity statements can and often do obscure institutional oppression such as racism. Such statements are often used as evidence that an institution does not have the kind of problems that diversity is supposed to solve. Ahmed, *On Being Included*.
41 Serano, *Whipping Girl*.
42 For an overview of these arguments, see American Civil Liberties Union, "Why Single-Sex Public Education Is a Civil Rights Issue"; American Psychological Association, "Single-Sex Education Unlikely to Offer Advantage."
43 Davis, "Transgressing the Masculine."
44 Mount Holyoke College, "Admission of Transgender Students."
45 Young, "Gender as Seriality."
46 Mount Holyoke College, "Admission of Transgender Students."

47 Common Application, "Apply to College."
48 Karkazis, *Fixing Sex.*
49 Sunstein and Thaler, *Nudge.*
50 Mill, "On Liberty."
51 Markovits and Bickford, "Constructing Freedom," 92.

CHAPTER 4. SEEING SEX IN THE BODY
 1 Levy, "Either/Or."
 2 Ibid.
 3 Sandel, "Case Against Perfection."
 4 Magubane, "Spectacles and Scholarship."
 5 Kendall, "Female Athletes Often Face the Femininity Police."
 6 Rankine, "Meaning of Serena Williams."
 7 Das, "Top Female Players."
 8 Dellinger, "Grass Ceiling."
 9 Rupert, "Genitals to Genes."
10 *Doping for Gold.*
11 Dreger, "Olympic Struggle over Sex."
12 Levy, "Either/Or."
13 Ubha, "Maria Sharapova Suspension."
14 The NCAA began including women's athletics only in the 1980s. Up until that point, women's intercollegiate athletics were regulated by the Association for Intercollegiate Athletics for Women (AIAW).
15 Griffin and Carroll, "NCAA Inclusion of Transgender Student-Athletes."
16 Thomas, "Transgender Man Playing Women's Basketball."
17 Griffin and Carroll, "NCAA Inclusion of Transgender Student-Athletes."
18 Ibid.
19 Serano, *Whipping Girl.*
20 For a good overview of the range of trans body experience, see Erickson-Schroth, *Trans Bodies, Trans Selves.*
21 Mill, *Subjection of Women.*
22 Currah, "New Transgender Panic."
23 By the time of the decision and court order, Maria Pepe was fourteen years old and no longer eligible to play Little League baseball.
24 Little League had good reason to believe that social custom and even the federal government endorsed its boys-only policy. In 1964, Congress issued Little League, Inc. a federal charter to "assist boys in developing qualities of citizenship, sportsmanship and manhood." Abrams, "Twelve-Year-Old Girl's Lawsuit."
25 Ibid.
26 Attorney General Opinion, Florida; *Lowenstein v. Amateur Softball Ass'n of America* (1988).
27 *Anderson v. Little League Baseball, Inc.* (1992).

28 *Martin v. PGA Tour, Inc.* (2000); *Matthews v. National Collegiate Athletic Association* (2001).
29 Bazelon and Hohenadel, "Cross-Court Winner."
30 Thomas, "Transgender Man Playing Women's Basketball."
31 *Moose Lodge no. 107 v. Irvis* (1972).
32 Hildebrand, "We Heart."
33 McDonagh and Pappano, *Playing with the Boys.*
34 Sandel, "Case Against Perfection."
35 For an analysis of the relationship between black masculinity and US sports, see Banet-Weiser, "Hoop Dreams."
36 Rankine, "Meaning of Serena Williams."
37 "Female Will Compete at Regional Combine for First Time."
38 "Lusia Harris."
39 Fuchs, "Manon Rheaume."
40 Canadian Press, "Canadian Women's Hockey Goalie."
41 Araton, "Mark Cuban's Offer."
42 This law applies to all levels of education, from preschool to postgraduate programs, and it also applies not just to students, but also to faculty and employees at educational institutions. Title IX covers "admissions, housing, course offerings, recruitment, financial assistance, counseling, student health, marital and parental status, insurance benefits, and harassment." Zaccone, "Policing the Policing of Intersex Bodies," 390n27. At the same time, there are numerous exemptions from Title IX, such as fraternities and sororities.
43 US Department of Justice and US Department of Education, "Dear Colleague Letter on Transgender Students."
44 Travers, "Queering Sport."

CONCLUSION

1 Andrew Flores finds that public attitudes toward transgender people, as with those toward lesbians and gay men, tend to increase with interpersonal contact. He notes that accurate data are difficult to collect because many people lack a clear sense of what transgender identities entail. See Flores, "Attitudes Toward Transgender Rights: Perceived Knowledge and Secondary Interpersonal Contact."
2 Butler, "Appearances Aside," 83.

REFERENCES

Abrams, Douglas E. "The Twelve-Year-Old Girl's Lawsuit That Changed America: The Continuing Impact of *NOW v. Little League Baseball, Inc.* at 40." *Virginia Journal of Social Policy & the Law* 20, no. 2 (2012): 241–69.

Adalman, Lori. "Prominent Women's Colleges Unwilling to Open Doors to Trans Women." *Feministing*, March 21, 2013. www.feministing.com.

Ahmed, Sara. *On Being Included: Racism and Diversity in Institutional Life.* Durham, NC: Duke University Press, 2012.

Alcoff, Linda Martin. *Visible Identities: Race, Gender, and the Self.* Oxford: Oxford University Press, 2005.

Allen, Jason. "A Quest for Acceptance: The Real ID Act and the Need for Comprehensive Gender Recognition Legislation in the United States." *Michigan Journal of Gender and Law* 14 (2008): 169–99.

American Civil Liberties Union. "Why Single-Sex Public Education Is a Civil Rights Issue." n.d. www.aclu.org.

American Psychological Association. "Single-Sex Education Unlikely to Offer Advantage over Coed Schools, Research Finds." Press release, February 3, 2014. www.apa.org.

Anderson v. Little League Baseball, Inc., 794 F. Supp. 342 (D. Ariz. 1992).

Anzalone, Christopher A. *U.S. Supreme Court Cases on Gender and Sexual Equality.* New York: Routledge, 2016.

Appiah, K. Anthony. "Stereotypes and the Shaping of Identity." In Post, *Prejudicial Appearances*, 55–72.

Araton, Harvey. "Mark Cuban's Offer Would Make Sideshow of Brittney Griner." *New York Times*, April 7, 2013. www.nytimes.com.

Arneil, Barbara. "Disability, Self-Image, and Modern Political Theory." *Political Theory* 37, no. 2 (2009): 218–42.

Associated Press. "Nicole Maines, Transgender Student, Goes to Maine High Court." *Huffington Post*, June 12, 2013. www.huffingtonpost.com.

———. "US Women's Colleges Change Admission Policies for Transgender Students." *Guardian*, September 10, 2014. www.theguardian.com.

Attorney General Opinion, Florida. Bill McCollum, attorney general of Florida. October 29, 2008. AGO, 2008–58 (Ops. Fla. Atty. Gen. 2008).

Australian Passport Office. "Sex and Gender Diverse Passport Applicants: Revised Policy." n.d. www.passports.gov.au.

Avi. "New York State Updates Birth Certificate Policy, Removing Surgical Requirement." Sylvia Rivera Law Project, June 5, 2014. www.srlp.org.

Banet-Weiser, Sarah. "Hoop Dreams: Professional Basketball and the Politics of Race and Gender." *Journal of Sport & Social Issues* 23, no. 4 (November 1, 1999): 403–20. doi:10.1177/0193723599234004.

Barnard College. "Admissions." http://admissions.barnard.edu.

Bazelon, Emily, and Kristin Hohenadel. "Cross-Court Winner." *Slate*, October 25, 2012. www.slate.com.

Beard, Katherine. "Germany: No Gender, No Problem on Birth Certificates." *U.S. News & World Report*, November 1, 2013. www.usnews.com.

Beauchamp, Toby, and Benjamin D'Harlingue. "Beyond Additions and Exceptions: The Category of Transgender and New Pedagogical Approaches for Women's Studies." *Feminist Formations* 24, no. 2 (2012): 25–51. doi:10.1353/ff.2012.0020.

Bennett College. "Bennett College Mission and Philosophy." August 23, 2016. www. bennett.edu.

Bickford, Susan. "Constructing Inequality: City Spaces and the Architecture of Citizenship." *Political Theory* 28, no. 3 (June 2000): 355–76.

Bornstein, Kate. *Gender Outlaw: On Men, Women, and the Rest of Us.* New York: Vintage, 1995.

Bowers v. Hardwick, 478 US 186 (1986).

Brase, Twila. "Not Just a Birth Certificate: How States Use Birth Certificates to Collect Data, Conduct Research and Warehouse Electronic Health Information." *Policy Insights*, February 2015. www.cchfreedom.org.

Brownstone, Sydney. "New Report Highlights Police Hostility toward Transgender Women of Color." *Village Voice*, June 4, 2013. www.villagevoice.com.

Brydum, Sunnivie. "N.J. Trans Woman Murdered, Media Misgenders Victim." *Advocate*, September 26, 2013. www.advocate.com.

Butler, Judith. "Appearances Aside." In Post, *Prejudicial Appearances*, 73–83.

———. *Undoing Gender.* New York: Routledge, 2004.

Butler, Judith, and Athena Athanasiou. *Dispossession: The Performative in the Political.* Cambridge: Polity, 2013.

California Department of Public Health. "Obtaining a New Birth Certificate after Gender Reassignment." January 2014. www.cdph.ca.gov.

Callahan, Kat. "Trans Women Offer Women's Colleges a New Way to Support an Old Mission." *ROYGBIV*, September 9, 2014. http://roygbiv.jezebel.com.

"Calliope Wong Discusses Smith College's Exclusion of Transgender Women on MSNBC." GLAAD, January 7, 2015. www.glaad.org/blog/

Canadian Press. "Canadian Women's Hockey Goalie Szabados Plans to Sign with Men's Pro Team." *Globe and Mail.* www.theglobeandmail.com.

Case, Mary Ann. "Why Not Abolish Laws of Urinary Segregation?" In Molotch and Noren, *Toilet*, 211–25.

Chen, Angus. "Health Effects of Transitioning in Teen Years Remain Unknown." NPR. www.npr.org.

Chodorow, Nancy. *Femininities, Masculinities, Sexualities: Freud and Beyond*. Lexington: University Press of Kentucky, 1994.

Colapinto, John. *As Nature Made Him: The Boy Who Was Raised as a Girl*. New York: HarperCollins, 2013.

Common Application. "Apply to College with the Common App." www.commonapp.org.

Coyote, Ivan E. "Fear and Loathing in Public Bathrooms, or How I Learned to Hold My Pee." *Slate*, April 11, 2014. www.slate.com.

Craig v. Boren, 429 F. Supp. 190 (1976).

Currah, Paisley. "The New Transgender Panic: Men in Women's Bathrooms." March 31, 2016. www.paisleycurrah.com.

Currah, Paisley, and Lisa Jean Moore. "'We Won't Know Who You Are': Contesting Sex Designations in New York City Birth Certificates." *Hypatia* 24, no. 3 (2009): 113–35.

Currah, Paisley, and Dean Spade. "The State We're In: Locations of Coercion and Resistance in Trans Policy, Part 2." *Sexuality Research and Social Policy* 5, no. 1 (2003): 1–4.

Das, Andrew. "Top Female Players Accuse U.S. Soccer of Wage Discrimination." *New York Times*, March 31, 2016. www.nytimes.com.

Davidson, Lee. "Bill Would Ban Transgender Bathroom Use in Schools." *Salt Lake Tribune*, January 31, 2014.

Davis, Georgiann. *Contesting Intersex: The Dubious Diagnosis*. New York: New York University Press, 2015.

Davis, James Earl. "Transgressing the Masculine: African American Boys and the Failure of Schools." In *What about the Boys? Issues of Masculinity in Schools*, edited by Wayne Martino and Bob Meyenn, 140–53. Philadelphia: Open University, 2001.

Dellinger, Hampton. "The Grass Ceiling: How to Conquer Inequality in Women's Soccer." *Atlantic*, July 5, 2015. www.theatlantic.com.

Denvir, Daniel. "SEPTA's Gender Discrimination: Is SEPTA Playing Gender Police?" *Philadelphia Weekly*, June 16, 2009. www.philadelphiaweekly.com.

Des Moines Register Editorial Board. "Editorial: Include Race on Licenses to Minimize Profiling." *Des Moines Register*, December 11, 2015. www.desmoinesregister.com.

Diamond, Morty. *From the Inside Out: Radical Gender Transformation, FTM and Beyond*. San Francisco: Manic D Press, 2004.

Doping for Gold. Directed by Alison Rooper. PBS/3BM Television, 2008.

Dreger, Alice. "The Olympic Struggle over Sex." *Atlantic*, July 2, 2012. www.theatlantic.com.

Erickson-Schroth, Laura. *Trans Bodies, Trans Selves: A Resource for the Transgender Community*. Oxford: Oxford University Press, 2014.

Fausto-Sterling, Anne. *Sexing the Body: Gender Politics and the Construct*. New York: Basic Books, 2000.

Feldman, Kiera. "Who Are Women's Colleges For?" *New York Times*, May 24, 2014. www.nytimes.com.

Feldman, Leonard. *Citizens without Shelter: Homelessness, Democracy, and Political Exclusion*. Ithaca, NY: Cornell University Press, 2006.

"Female Will Compete at Regional Combine for First Time." February 19, 2013. www. nfl.com.

Finn, Jonathan. *Capturing the Criminal Image: From Mug Shot to Surveillance Society*. Minneapolis: University of Minnesota Press, 2009.

Flores, Andrew. "Attitudes toward Transgender Rights: Perceived Knowledge and Secondary Interpersonal Contact." *Politics, Groups, and Identities* 3, no. 3 (2015): 398–416.

Frank, Gillian. "The Anti-trans Bathroom Nightmare Has Its Roots in Racial Segregation." *Slate*, November 10, 2015. www.slate.com.

Friedan, Betty. *The Feminine Mystique*. 50th anniversary ed. New York: Norton, 2013.

Frosch, Dan. "In Colorado, a Legal Dispute over Transgender Rights." *New York Times*, March 17, 2013. www.nytimes.com.

Fuchs, Jeremy. "Manon Rheaume, NHL's First Female Goalie, Continues to Inspire." *Sports Illustrated*, June 27, 2016. www.si.com.

Gay, Roxane. "The Seduction of Safety, on Campus and Beyond." *New York Times*, November 13, 2015. www.nytimes.com.

Geidner, Chris. "Federal Officials Protect Transgender Student Against Discrimination." *BuzzFeed*, July 24, 2013. www.buzzfeed.com.

———. "Transgender Breakthrough." *Metro Weekly*, April 23, 2012. www.metroweekly. com.

General Assembly of North Carolina. "Session Law 2016–3 House Bill 2." March 23, 2016. www.ncleg.net.

"Girl, 7, Raped and Slain at a Casino in Nevada." *New York Times*, May 29, 1997. www. nytimes.com.

Goldberg, Michelle. "What Is a Woman? The Dispute between Radical Feminism and Transgenderism." *New Yorker*, August 4, 2014.

Grant, Jamie M., Lisa A. Mottet, Justin Tanis, Jack Harrison, Jody L. Herman, and Mara Keisling. "Injustice at Every Turn: A Report of the National Transgender Discrimination Survey." Washington, DC: National Gay and Lesbian Task Force and the National Center for Transgender Equality, 2011. www.thetaskforce.org.

Greed, Clara. "Creating a Nonsexist Restroom." In Molotch and Noren, *Toilet*, 117–41.

Griffin, Pat, and Helen Carroll. "NCAA Inclusion of Transgender Student-Athletes." Indianapolis, IN: National Collegiate Athletics Association, August 2011.

Halberstam, Judith. *Female Masculinity*. Durham, NC: Duke University Press, 1998.

Hampden-Sydney College. "Hampden-Sydney College Mission Statement." August 23, 2016. www.hsc.edu.

Hamraie, Aimi. "Designing Collective Access: A Feminist Disability Theory of Universal Design." *Disability Studies Quarterly* 33, no. 4 (2013). http://dsq-sds.org

Harris, Elizabeth A. "Barnard College, After Much Discussion, Decides to Accept Transgender Women." *New York Times*, June 4, 2015. www.nytimes.com.

Hauser, Philip M. "The President's Column." *American Statistician* 16, no. 2 (1962): 1–24.

Haywood, Mari. "Update: Diamond Williams, Transgender Woman Murdered in Philadelphia." GLAAD, July 23, 2013. www.glaad.org.

Hennessey, Rachel. "What's in a Women's College?" *Forbes*, February 6, 2013. www.forbes.com.

Herman, Jody L. "Gendered Restrooms and Minority Stress: The Public Regulation of Gender and Its Impact on Transgender People's Lives." *Journal of Public Management and Social Policy* 19, no. 1 (2013): 65–80.

Hildebrand, James. "We Heart: Mo'ne Davis, Little League Pitcher." *Ms. Magazine*, August 11, 2014. www.msmagazine.com.

Hillman, Thea. *Intersex (for Lack of a Better Word)*. San Francisco: Manic D Press, 2008.

Huppke, Rex W. "Transgender People Sue Illinois to Change Birth Certificates." *Chicago Tribune*, May 12, 2011. www.chicagotribune.com.

Intersex Society of North America. "How Common Is Intersex?" n.d. www.isna.org.

———. "Our Mission." n.d. www.isna.org.

Jaschik, Scott. "Affirmative Action for Men." *Inside Higher Education*, March 27, 2006. www.insidehighered.com.

———. "2 Christian Colleges Win Title IX Exemptions That Give Them the Right to Expel Transgender Students." *Inside Higher Ed*, July 25, 2014. www.insidehighered.com.

Karkazis, Katrina. *Fixing Sex: Intersex, Medical Authority, and Lived Experience*. Durham, NC: Duke University Press, 2008.

Kendall, Erika Nicole. "Female Athletes Often Face the Femininity Police—Especially Serena Williams." *Guardian*, July 14, 2015. www.theguardian.com.

King, Aliya S. "The Mean Girls of Morehouse." *Vibe*, October 11, 2010. www.vibe.com.

Kirkland, Anna. "What's at Stake in Transgender Discrimination as Sex Discrimination?" *Signs* 32, no. 1 (2006): 83–111. doi:10.1086/signs.2006.32.issue-1.

Kogan, Terry. "Sex Separation: The Cure-All for Victorian Social Anxiety." In Molotch and Noren, *Toilet*, 145–64.

Kohn, Margaret. *Brave New Neighborhoods: The Privatization of Public Space*. New York: Routledge, 2004.

Lacqueur, Thomas. *Making Sex: Body and Gender from the Greeks to Freud*. Cambridge, MA: Harvard University Press, 1992.

Lawrence v. Texas, 539 US 558 (2003).

Lee, Jennifer. "Sexual Stereotypes, Civil Rights and a Suit about Both." *New York Times*, October 10, 2007. www.nytimes.com.

———. "Woman Wins a Settlement over Her Bathroom Ouster." *New York Times*, May 14, 2008. www.nytimes.com.

Lee, Jennifer, and Min Zhou. *The Asian American Achievement Paradox*. New York: Russell Sage Foundation, 2015.

Leff, Lisa. "Transgender ID Cards: Are the 'M' and 'F' Outdated?" *Huffington Post*, June 15, 2013. www.huffingtonpost.com.

Levy, Ariel. "Either/Or: Sports, Sex, and the Case of Caster Semenya." *New Yorker*, November 23, 2009. www.newyorker.com.

Link, Aaron Raz, and Hilda Raz. *What Becomes You*. Lincoln: University of Nebraska Press, 2008.

Lovehall, Christian A'Xavier. "Passing as a Transsexual Black Man, and the Revolutionary Courage to Continue." *NewsWorks*, August 13, 2015. www.newsworks.org.

Lowenstein v. Amateur Softball Ass'n of America, 418 N.W. 2d 231 (Neb. 1988).

"Lusia Harris: The First Woman NBA Player." *NBA Hoops Online*, n.d. www.nbahoopsonline.com.

Lyon, David. *Identifying Citizens: ID Cards as Surveillance*. Cambridge: Polity, 2009.

MacKinnon, Catharine A. *Feminism Unmodified: Discourses on Life and Law*. Cambridge, MA: Harvard University Press, 1988.

Magubane, Zine. "Spectacles and Scholarship: Caster Semenya, Intersex Studies, and the Problem of Race in Feminist Theory." *Signs* 39, no. 3 (2014): 761–85.

Malone, Michael. "Gender Benders." *Restaurant Business* 103, no. 11 (July 15, 2004): 38–42.

Marder, Dianna. "Transgender Riders Seek Justice from SEPTA." *Philly-Archives*, February 28, 2011. http://articles.philly.com.

Markovits, Elizabeth Ka., and Susan Bickford. "Constructing Freedom: Institutional Pathways to Changing the Gender Division of Labor." *Perspectives on Politics* 12, no. 1 (March 2014): 81–99. doi:10.1017/S1537592713003721.

Marso, Lori J. "Feminism's Quest for Common Desires." *Perspectives on Politics* 8, no. 1 (2010): 263–69.

Martin v. PGA Tour, Inc., 204 F.3d 994 (9th Cir. 2000).

Matthews v. National Collegiate Athletic Association, 179 F. Supp. 1209 (E.D. Wash 2001).

McDonagh, Eileen, and Laura Pappano. *Playing with the Boys: Why Separate Is Not Equal in Sports*. Oxford: Oxford University Press, 2009.

Mill, John Stuart. "On Liberty." In *Mill: Texts, Commentaries*, edited by Alan Ryan, 41–131. New York: Norton, 1997.

———. *The Subjection of Women*. Rev. ed. Mineola, NY: Dover, 1997.

Molotch, Harvey, and Laura Noren, eds. *Toilet: Public Restrooms and the Politics of Sharing*. New York: New York University Press, 2010.

Moose Lodge no. 107 v. Irvis, 407 US 163 (1972).

Moran, Tim. "Evanston Becomes 7th U.S. City to Adopt Gender-Neutral Restroom Signs." *Evanston Patch*, November 13, 2015. www.patch.com.

Morehouse College. "Morehouse College Mission." August 23, 2016. www.morehouse.edu.

Mottet, Lisa. "Modernizing State Vital Statistics Statutes and Policies to Ensure Accurate Gender Markers on Birth Certificates: A Good Government Approach to

Recognizing the Lives of Transgender People." *Michigan Journal of Gender and Law* 19 (2013): 373–470.

Mount Holyoke College. "Admission of Transgender Students." n.d. www.mtholyoke. edu.

Muller, Benjamin J. *Security, Risk and the Biometric State: Governing Borders and Bodies.* New York: Routledge, 2010.

National Center for Transgender Equality. "Department of Homeland Security REAL ID Final Regulations." March 13, 2008. www.transequality.org.

NBC10 and Wire Reports. "Gender-Neutral Restrooms Become the Law." *NBC 10 Philadelphia*, November 5, 2013. www.nbcphiladelphia.com.

New York City Human Rights Law. Administrative Code of the City of New York. Title 8. www1.nyc.gov.

"New York Ousts 'Race' from Forms." *New Pittsburgh Courier*, January 7, 1961.

New York State Human Rights Law. Public Accommodations. https://dhr.ny.gov.

New York Times Editorial Board. "Transgender Law Makes North Carolina Pioneer in Bigotry." *New York Times*, March 25, 2016. www.nytimes.com.

Nussbaum, Paul. "City to Probe Transit Rider's Gender ID Complaint." *Philly-Archives*, September 20, 2008. http://articles.philly.com.

Okin, Susan Moller. *Justice, Gender, and the Family.* Repr. ed. New York: Basic Books, 1991.

Padawer, Ruth. "When Women Become Men at Wellesley." *New York Times*, October 15, 2014. www.nytimes.com.

Philadelphia Commission on Human Relations. "Public Accommodations Discrimination." n.d. www.phila.gov.

Pieklo, Jessica. "Illinois Consent Decree Important Step for Transgender Individuals Seeking Birth Certificate Changes." *Rewire*, October 26, 2012. http://rewire.news.

Post, Robert C., ed. *Prejudicial Appearances: The Logic of American Antidiscrimination Law.* Durham, NC: Duke University Press, 2001.

"Putting a Face to Calliope Wong." *Snowflake Especial*, March 21, 2013. http://snowflakeespecial.tumblr.com.

Quart, Alissa. "When Girls Will Be Boys." *New York Times Magazine*, March 16, 2008. www.nytimes.com.

Rankine, Claudia. "The Meaning of Serena Williams: On Tennis and Black Excellence." *New York Times*, August 25, 2015. www.nytimes.com.

REAL ID Act. Pub. L. No. 109–13, 119 Stat. 231 (2005).

Regents of the University of California v. Bakke, 438 US 265 (1978).

Riders Against Gender Exclusion. "R.A.G.E.: About Us." n.d. https://phillyrage.wordpress.com.

Ring, Trudy. "This Year's Michigan Womyn's Music Festival Will Be the Last." *Advocate*, April 21, 2015. www.advocate.com.

Roberts, Dorothy. *Fatal Intervention: How Science, Politics, and Big Business Re-create Race in the Twenty-First Century.* New York: New Press, 2011.

———. *Killing the Black Body: Race, Reproduction and the Meaning of Liberty*. New York: Random House/Pantheon, 1997.

Robertson, Craig. *The Passport in America: The History of a Document*. Oxford: Oxford University Press, 2010.

Rubin Erdely, Sabrina. "The Six-Year-Old Who Wants to Change Gender." *Rolling Stone*, October 28, 2013. www.rollingstone.com.

Rupert, James L. "Genitals to Genes: The History and Biology of Gender Verification in the Olympics." *Canadian Bulletin of Medical History* 28, no. 2 (2011): 339–65.

Sacramento County Health and Human Services. "Out-of-Hospital Birth Registration." 2016. www.dhhs.saccounty.net.

Sandel, Michael J. "The Case Against Perfection." *Atlantic*, April 2004. www.theatlantic.com.

Scott, James C. *Seeing Like a State: How Certain Schemes to Improve the Human Condition Have Failed*. New Haven, CT: Yale University Press, 1998.

Serano, Julia. *Whipping Girl: A Transsexual Woman on Sexism and the Scapegoating of Femininity*. Berkeley, CA: Seal Press, 2009.

Sheridan, Mary Beth, and Ed O'Keefe. "Parentage Goes 'Gender Neutral' on Passport Form." *Washington Post*, January 8, 2011. www.washingtonpost.com.

Shrage, Laurie. "Does the Government Need to Know Your Sex?" *Journal of Political Philosophy* 20, no. 2 (2012): 225–47.

Silber, Chad. "McCrory Defends Controversial New Law." *WFMY News*, March 24, 2016. www.wfmynews2.com.

Smith College. "About Smith." www.smith.edu.

Snorton, C. Riley. "'A New Hope': The Psychic Life of Passing." *Hypatia* 24, no. 3 (2009): 77–92. doi:10.1111/j.1527–2001.2009.01046.x.

Southeastern Pennsylvania Transportation Authority. "Board Approves Fare Increases; Budget Action Deferred." May 23, 2013. www.septa.org.

Spade, Dean. "Documenting Gender." *Hastings Law Journal* 59 (2008): 731–841.

———. "Keynote Address: Trans Law & Politics on a Neoliberal Landscape." *Temple Political & Civil Rights Law Review* 18 (2009): 353–73.

Spelman College. "Spelman College Mission Statement." n.d. www.spelman.edu.

Stanton, Elizabeth Cady. *Solitude of Self*. Ashfield, MA: Paris Press, 2000.

———. *The Woman's Bible*. Lebanon, NH: Northeastern University Press, 1993.

Sunstein, Cass, and Richard Thaler. *Nudge: Improving Decisions about Health, Wealth and Happiness*. New Haven, CT: Yale University Press, 2009.

Sycamore, Mattilda Bernstein. *That's Revolting! Queer Strategies for Resisting Assimilation*. Berkeley, CA: Soft Skull Press, 2004.

Thomas, Katie. "Transgender Man Playing Women's Basketball at George Washington." *New York Times*, November 1, 2010. www.nytimes.com.

Thompson, Debra. *The Schematic State: Race, Transnationalism, and the Politics of the Census*. New York: Cambridge University Press, 2016.

Threadcraft, Shatema. "The Black Female Body at the Intersection of State Failure and Necropower." *Contemporary Political Theory* 15, no. 1 (2016): 105–9.

Transgender Law Center. "DMV Again Settles with a Transgender Woman Assaulted in Bay Area." June 4, 2015. www.transgenderlawcenter.org.

———. "Kansas Woman Sues State for Denying Her an Accurate Birth Certificate." February 24, 2016. www.transgenderlawcenter.org.

Transpass. Directed by Wren Warner. www.vimeo.com/48770346.

Travers, Ann. "Queering Sport: Lesbian Softball Leagues and the Transgender Challenge." *International Review for the Sociology of Sport* 41, nos. 3–4 (2006): 431–46.

Tronto, Joan C. *Caring Democracy: Markets, Equality, and Justice*. New York: New York University Press, 2013.

Ubha, Ravi. "Maria Sharapova Suspension: Banned for Two Years." *CNN.com*, July 1, 2016. http://edition.cnn.com.

United States v. Carolene Products Company, 304 US 144 (1938).

United States v. Virginia, 518 US 515 (1996).

US Department of Education. "Title IX and Sex Discrimination." October 15, 2015. www2.ed.gov.

US Department of Justice. "Guidance on the 2010 ADA Standards for Accessible Design: Volume 2." September 15, 2010. www.ada.gov.

US Department of Justice, Civil Rights Division. "Advisory, Toilet Rooms and Bathing Rooms, Americans with Disabilities Standards for Accessible Design." 2010. www.ada.gov.

US Department of Justice and US Department of Education. "Dear Colleague Letter on Transgender Students." May 13, 2016. www.justice.gov.

US Department of State. "How to Apply for a Passport." n.d. http://travel.state.gov.

———. "New Policy on Gender Change in Passports Announced." June 9, 2010. www.state.gov.

Wabash College. "Wabash College Mission Statement." August 23, 2016. www.wabash.edu.

Waldron, Jeremy. "Homelessness and the Issue of Freedom." In *Contemporary Political Philosophy: An Anthology*, edited by Robert E. Goodin and Philip Pettit, 432–48. Malden, MA: Blackwell, 2006.

Wollstonecraft, Mary. *A Vindication of the Rights of Woman*. 2nd ed. Mineola, NY: Dover, 1996.

Young, Iris. "Gender as Seriality: Thinking about Women as a Social Collective." *Signs* 19, no. 3 (Spring 1994): 713–38.

Zaccone, Laura A. "Policing the Policing of Intersex Bodies: Softening the Lines in Title IX Athletic Programs." *Brooklyn Law Review* 76, no. 1 (2010): 385–438.

INDEX

Bold page numbers refer to figures/tables

ABOUT THE AUTHOR

Heath Fogg Davis is Associate Professor of Political Science at Temple University. He is the author of *The Ethics of Transracial Adoption*.

5/17